Crimson Short W

Snowdonia

Compiled by Terry Marsh

Text: Terry Marsh
Photography: Terry Marsh
Editorial: Ark Creative (UK) Ltd
Design: Ark Creative (UK) Ltd

ISBN: 978-1-85458-524-0

While every care has been taken to ensure the accuracy of the route directions, the publishers cannot accept responsibility for errors or omissions, or for changes in details

If you find an inaccuracy in either the text or maps, please write to Crimson Publishing at the address below.

First published 2003
Revised and reprinted 2008, 2010.

This edition first published in Great Britain 2010 by Crimson Publishing, a division of:
Crimson Business Ltd
Westminster House, Kew Road
Richmond, Surrey, TW9 2ND

www.totalwalking.co.uk

Printed in Singapore. 5/10

A catalogue record for this book is available from the British library.

wy Castle and Estuary
ıntain
3eddgelert

Contents

Keymap 1

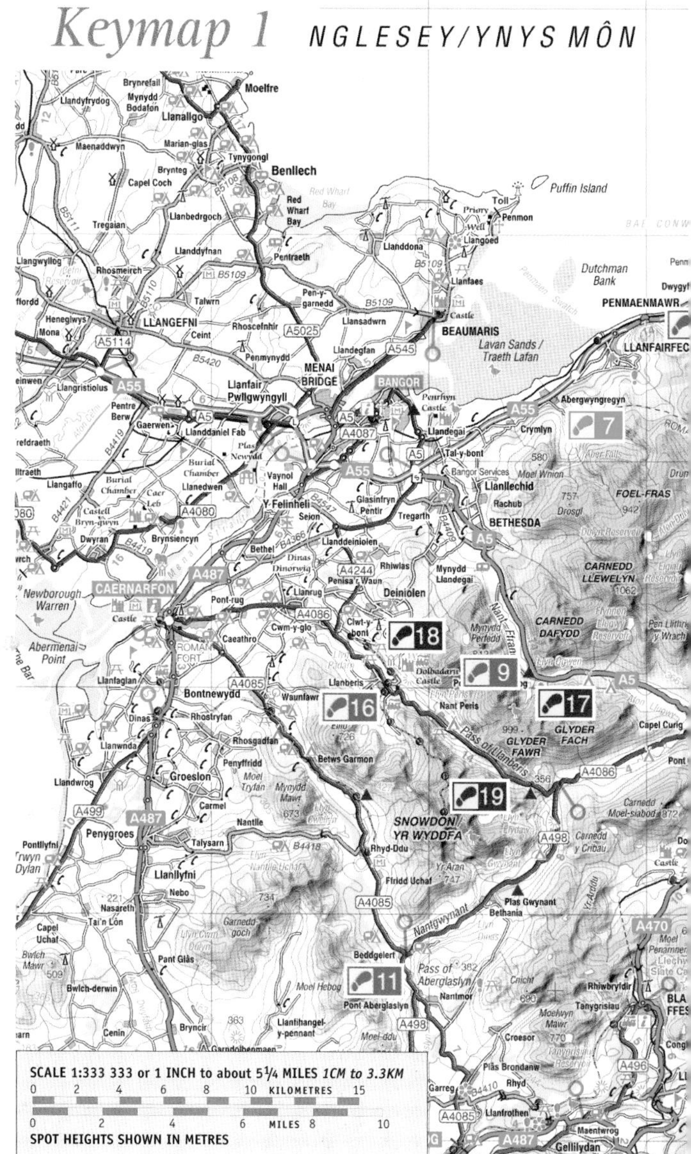
ANGLESEY/YNYS MÔN
Moelfre
Brynrefail
Mynydd Bodafon
Llandyfrydog
Llanallgo
Maenaddwyn
Marian-glas
Tynygongl
Benllech
Brynteg
Capel Coch
Red Wharf Bay
Red Wharf Bay
Llanbedrgoch
Tregaian
Puffin Island
Toll
Priory
Penmon
Well
Llangoed
Llanddona
Llanfaes
Llanddyfnan
Pentraeth
Llangwyllog
Rhosmeirch
Cefni Reservoir
Talwrn
Pen-y-garnedd
Llansadwrn
Castle
BEAUMARIS
Dutchman Bank
Penmaen Swatch
BAE CONWY
PENMAENMAWR
LLANFAIRFEC
Heneglwys
Mona
LLANGEFNI
Ceint
Rhoscefnhir
Penmynydd
Llandegfan
Lavan Sands / Traeth Lafan
MENAI BRIDGE
BANGOR
Llanfair Pwllgwyngyll
Llangristiolus
Pentre Berw
Gaerwen
Llanddaniel Fab
Plas Newydd
Penrhyn Castle
Llandegai
Abergwyngregyn
Crymlyn
Aber Falls
Tal-y-bont
Bangor Services
Moel Wnion
Llanllechid
Rachub
Drosgl
FOEL-FRAS
BETHESDA
Burial Chamber
Burial Chamber
Caer Leb
Llangaffo
Llanedwen
Vaynol Hall
Y Felinheli
Glasinfryn
Pentir
Tregarth
Seion
Castell Bryn-gwyn
Dwyran
Brynsiencyn
Menai Strait
Bethel
Dinas Dinorwig
Llanddeiniolen
Rhiwlas
Mynydd Llandegai
CARNEDD LLEWELYN
Newborough Warren
CAERNARFON
Castle
Penisa'r Waun
Llanrug
Deiniolen
Pont-rug
Cwm-y-glo
Clwt-y-bont
Abermenai Point
Caeathro
ROMAN FORT
Mynydd Perfedd
Nant Ffrancon
CARNEDD DAFYDD
Llyn Ogwen
Dolbadarn Castle
Llanfaglan
Bontnewydd
Llanberis
Waunfawr
Llyn Peris
Nant Peris
Dinas
Rhostryfan
GLYDER FAWR
GLYDER FACH
Capel Curig
Llanwnda
Rhosgadfan
Pass of Llanberis
Betws Garmon
Penyffridd
Moel Tryfan
Mynydd Mawr
Llandwrog
Groeslon
Carmel
Nantlle
Carnedd Moel-siabod
SNOWDON/YR WYDDFA
Penygroes
Talysarn
Rhyd-Ddu
Carnedd y Cribau
Pontllyfni
Llanllyfni
Nebo
Yr Aran
Ffridd Uchaf
Nasareth
Plas Gwynant
Bethania
Tai'n Lôn
Nantgwynant
Capel Uchaf
Garnedd-goch
Bwlch Mawr
Pant Glâs
Beddgelert
Pass of Aberglaslyn
Cnicht
Rhiwbryfdir
Bwlch-derwin
Moel Hebog
Pont Aberglaslyn
Nantmor
Tanygrisiau
Moelwyn Mawr
Bryncir
Llanfihangel-y-pennant
Moel-ddu
Croesor
Cenin
Garndolbenmaen
Plâs Brondanw
Garreg
Rhyd
Llanfrothen
Maentwrog
Gellilydan
SCALE 1:333 333 or 1 INCH to about 5¼ MILES 1CM to 3.3KM
KILOMETRES
MILES
SPOT HEIGHTS SHOWN IN METRES

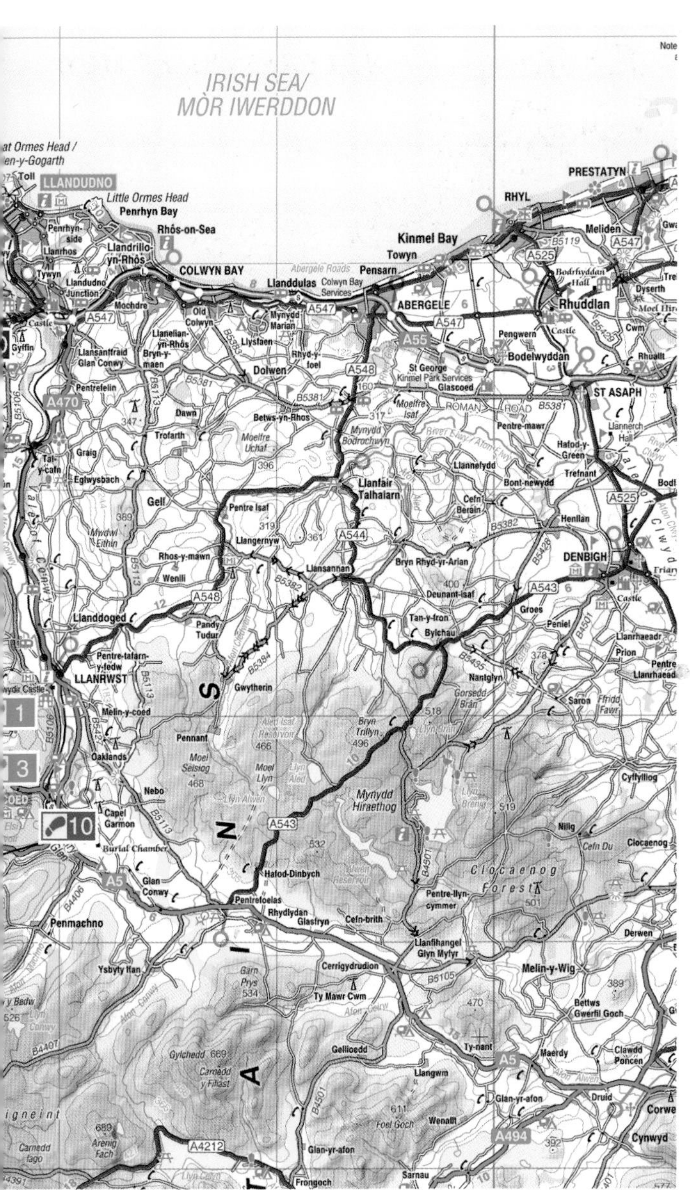
IRISH SEA/
MÒR IWERDDON
LLANDUDNO
Little Ormes Head
Penrhyn Bay
Rhôs-on-Sea
COLWYN BAY
Llanddulas
Pensarn
Towyn
Kinmel Bay
RHYL
PRESTATYN
ABERGELE
Rhuddlan
Bodelwyddan
ST ASAPH
Llanfair Talhaiarn
Llangernyw
Llansannan
DENBIGH
LLANRWST
Gwytherin
Mynydd Hiraethog
Clocaenog Forest
Pentrefoelas
Cerrigydrudion
Melin-y-Wig
Penmachno
Ysbyty Ifan
Frongoch
Corwen
Cynwyd

Keymap 2

A498
A487
A497
A4085
A496
A493
B4410
B4573
B4405
Golan
Moel-ddu
552
Croesor
Plâs Brondanw
Garreg
Rhyd
Llanfrothen
Maentwrog
Gellilydan
Penrhyndeudraeth
Well
Llangybi
Rhoslan
Llanarmon
Llanystumdwy
Chwilog
Gell
Pentrefelin
Penmorfa
Tremadog
Prenteg
PORTHMADOG
Castle
262
Minffordd
Toll
Cilfor
CRICCIETH
Holiday Camp
Pen-ychain
Morfa Bychan
Borth-y-Gest
Portmeirion
Traeth Bach
Talsarnau
Ynys
Eisingrug
Morfa Harlech
BAE TREMADOG
Harlech
Castle
380
623
Moel Ysgyfarnogod
Craig Ddrwg
Cwm Bychan
Roman Steps
Rhinog Fawr
720
Llanfair
Llandanwg
Pen-sarn
Pentre Gwynfryn
Llanbedr
Cwm Nantcol
Y Llethr
754
589
Moelfre
Morfa Dyffryn
Coed Ystumgwern
750
Diffwys
Llanenddwyn
Dyffryn Ardudwy
Burial Chambers
Llanddwywe
Tal-y-bont
Llawlech
Uwch-mynydd
Pen-y-bryn
15
Toll
Caerdeon
Llanaber
Cutiau
Penmaenpool
Abergwyn
BARMOUTH
Islawr-dref
383
BARMOUTH BAY/ BAE BERMO
The Bar
Arthog
Fairbourne
CADA
622
Mynydd Pennant
Llwyngwril
Esgair Berfa
Castell y Bere
Llanfihangel-y-pennant
5
Llangelynnin
Rhoslefain
Abergyno
Mynydd Tan-y-coed
Tarrenhendre
633
Llanfendigaid
Tonfanau
35
Llanegryn
309
Dolgoch
Bryncrug
Bryngias Station
Aber Dysynni
Broad Water
Pen Trum-gwr
Rhyd-yr-onen
Trum Gelli
Pennal
Cwrt
19
TYWYN
Corlan Fraith
Caethle
4
SCALE 1:312 500 or 1 INCH to 5 MILES 1CM to 3.1 KM
0 2 4 6 8 10 KILOMETRES 15
0 2 4 6 MILES 8 10
SPOT HEIGHTS SHOWN IN METRES

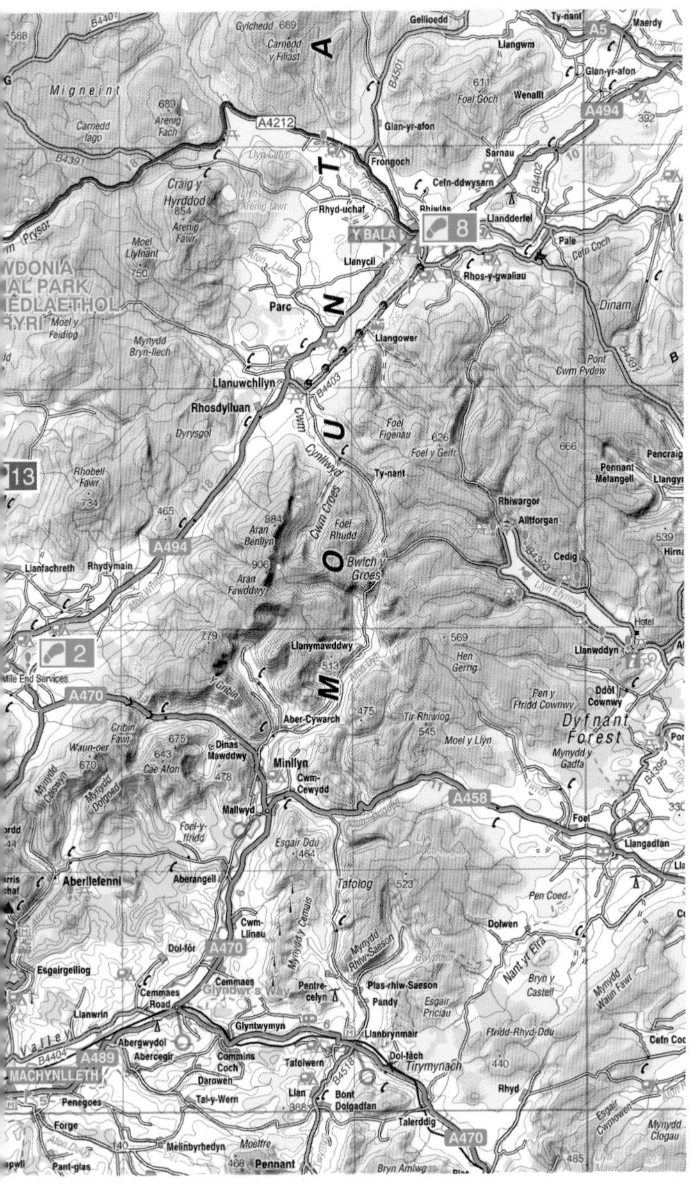

At-a-glance

Short walks up to 3½ miles

1	2	3	4

Llyn Geirionydd	*Llwybr Clywedog (Torrent Walk)*	*Afon Llugwy and the Miners' Bridge*	*Llyn Barfog*
• **Woodland wildlife** • **monument** • **waterfowl** • **lakeside path**	• **Woodland trail** • **wild flowers** • **cascades** • **gated lane**	• **Odd bridge** • **river gorge** • **woodland birdlife** • **riverside picnics**	• **Enchanted lake** • **superb views** • **legends** • **King Arthur**
Walk Distance 2 miles (3.2km) **Time** 1 hour **Refreshments** None	**Walk Distance** 2 miles (3.2km) **Time** 1 hour **Refreshments** Dolgellau	**Walk Distance** 2¼ miles (3.8km) **Time** 1 hour **Refreshments** Café at station and along A5	**Walk Distance** 2 miles (3.2km) **Time** 1 hour **Refreshments** None
Woodland; lakeside path has slippery tree roots and rocks and *care is required*	Woodland trails; rocky steps; gated road	Woodland trails and paths; riverside paths; forest road	Farm tracks; upland paths; stiles; old mine workings
p. 18	p. 22	p. 25	p. 29
Walk Completed ☐	Walk Completed ☐	Walk Completed ☐	Walk Completed ☐

5

Castell y Bere

- Ancient castle
- Mary Jones' home
- attractive church
- beautiful valley

Walk Distance
2 miles (3.2km)
Time
1 hour
Refreshments
Pubs in Abergynolwyn

Field paths and tracks (very muddy); narrow lanes; stiles

p.33

Walk Completed ☐

6

Coed Ganllwyd

- Forest wildlife
- waterfalls
- gold mine
- picnic area

Walk Distance
2½ miles (4km)
Time
1½ hours
Refreshments
Dolgellau

Woodland paths; upland trails; ladder-stiles; slippery rocks

p. 37

Walk Completed ☐

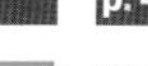

7

Aber Falls

- Varied birdlife
- Welsh tyddyn
- waterfalls
- nature reserve

Walk Distance
2¾ miles (4.5km)
Time
1½ to 2 hours
Refreshments
Pub in Aber

Riverside paths; woodland trails; stiles

p. 41

Walk Completed ☐

8

Bala Lake

- Glorious views
- waterfowl
- railway
- lakeshore picnics

Walk Distance
3½ miles (5.8km)
Time
2 hours
Refreshments
Bala

Woodland trails; farm paths; roads

p. 45

Walk Completed ☐

Slightly harder walks of 3 to 5 miles

9	10	11	12

 *Cwm Idwal*	*Llyn Elsi*	*Sygun and Llyn Dinas*	*Llyn Gwernan*
• Mountain birdlife • glacial lake • rock climbers • mountain scenery	• Mixed woodland • waterfowl • mountain lake • forest wildlife	• Attractive village • old copper mine • mountains • excellent views	• Upland birdlife • ancient road • beautiful scenery • wooded lakeside
Walk Distance 3 miles (4.7km) **Time** 2 hours **Refreshments** Snack bar at start	**Walk Distance** 3 miles (4.7km) **Time** 2 hours **Refreshments** Café at station	**Walk Distance** 3½ miles (5.8km) **Time** 2–3 hours **Refreshments** Pubs and cafés in Beddgelert	**Walk Distance** 3½ miles (5.6km) **Time** 2 hours **Refreshments** Gwernan Lake Hotel
Rough bouldery paths; rocky terrain; ladder-stiles	Woodland trails and paths; lakeside paths	Riverside trails; mountain uplands; *two significant ascents*	Lakeside paths; ancient road; stiles; farm tracks; some uphill
p. 50	p. 54	p. 58	p. 63
Walk Completed ☐	Walk Completed ☐	Walk Completed ☐	Walk Completed ☐ 

13	14	15	16

Coed-y-Brenin	*Above Penmaenmawr*	*Mawddach Estuary*	*Yr Wyddfa (Snowdon)*
• Woodland wildlife • waterfalls • gold mine • forest trails	• Upland flora • prehistoric cairns • stone circle • wild ponies	• Estuarine wildlife • railway trackbed • woodland wildlife • craggy upland	• Mountain railway • rugged scenery • stupendous views • mountain summit
Walk Distance 3½ miles (5.6km)	**Walk Distance** 4 miles (6.5km)	**Walk Distance** 5 miles (8km)	**Walk Distance** 4¾ miles (7.5km)
Time 2 hours	**Time** 2 hours	**Time** 2–3 hours	**Time** 2 hours
Refreshments Dolgellau	**Refreshments** Pubs and cafés in Conwy and Dwygyfylchi	**Refreshments** Penmaenpool	**Refreshments** Llanberis and at Snowdon summit
Broad woodland tracks; footbridges; road walking	Hill tracks and paths; ladder-stiles; vehicle tracks	Estuary; woodland; mountain upland; farmland	High mountain paths; steep slopes; loose stones
p.68	p. 72	p. 76	p. 81
Walk Completed ☐	Walk Completed ☐	Walk Completed ☐	Walk Completed ☐

Walks with steeper ascents of 4½ miles or more

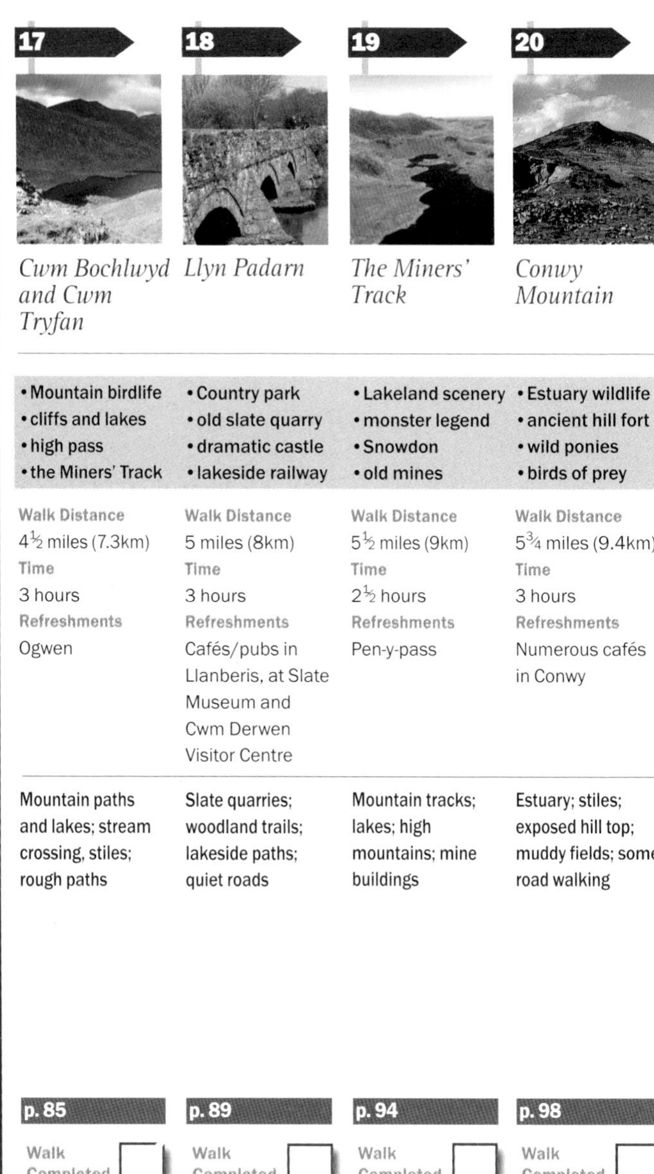

17	18	19	20
Cwm Bochlwyd and Cwm Tryfan	*Llyn Padarn*	*The Miners' Track*	*Conwy Mountain*
• Mountain birdlife • cliffs and lakes • high pass • the Miners' Track	• Country park • old slate quarry • dramatic castle • lakeside railway	• Lakeland scenery • monster legend • Snowdon • old mines	• Estuary wildlife • ancient hill fort • wild ponies • birds of prey
Walk Distance 4½ miles (7.3km)	**Walk Distance** 5 miles (8km)	**Walk Distance** 5½ miles (9km)	**Walk Distance** 5¾ miles (9.4km)
Time 3 hours	**Time** 3 hours	**Time** 2½ hours	**Time** 3 hours
Refreshments Ogwen	**Refreshments** Cafés/pubs in Llanberis, at Slate Museum and Cwm Derwen Visitor Centre	**Refreshments** Pen-y-pass	**Refreshments** Numerous cafés in Conwy
Mountain paths and lakes; stream crossing, stiles; rough paths	Slate quarries; woodland trails; lakeside paths; quiet roads	Mountain tracks; lakes; high mountains; mine buildings	Estuary; stiles; exposed hill top; muddy fields; some road walking
p. 85	p. 89	p. 94	p. 98
Walk Completed ☐	Walk Completed ☐	Walk Completed ☐	Walk Completed ☐

Introduction

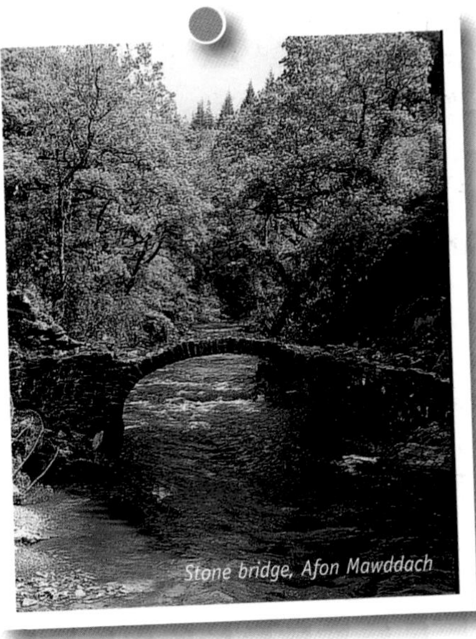
Stone bridge, Afon Mawddach

The routes and information in this book have been devised specifically with families and children in mind. All the walks include points of interest as well as a question to provide an objective.

If you, or your children, have not walked before, choose from the shorter walks for your first outings, although only one of the walks is especially demanding. The purpose is not simply to get from A to B, but to enjoy an exploration, which may be just a steady stroll in the countryside, alongside rivers and lakes, or at the edge of mountains.

The walks are graded by length and difficulty, but few landscapes are truly flat, something of a rarity in Snowdonia, so even short walks may involve some ascent, although nowhere is this excessive. Details are given under Route Features in the first information box for each route. But the precise nature of the ground underfoot will depend on recent weather conditions. If you do set out on a walk and discover the going is harder than you expected, or the weather has deteriorated, do not be afraid to turn back. The route will always be there another day, when you are fitter or the children are more experienced or the weather is better. Almost all the walks involve some measure of rough terrain or steep grassy slopes, making it advisable to wear proper walking footwear rather than trainers or wellington boots. Some are not suitable for cloudy days.

Bear in mind that the countryside changes. Landmarks may disappear, gates may become stiles, rights of way may be altered. In a few places the terrain can be confusing, and this means having to pay rather close attention to route descriptions and waymarking or, in the absence of waymarking, the general direction followed by the path.

A few of the walks venture into truly mountainous terrain, at a low level, but it seems strange to produce a book, even of short walks, without paying a visit to the top of Snowdon. To make life easier, this walk makes use of the Snowdon Mountain Railway to reach the highest summit in England and Wales, leaving you simply to walk down to Llanberis.

Snowdonia

Generally, although incorrectly, only the mountain ranges in the extreme north west of Wales are known by the name Snowdonia. In fact, Snowdonia, in the guise of a National Park, covers a much larger area of 827 square miles and extends far south to Bala, Dolgellau and beyond: this book does the same, and offers walks in

At Mawddach

all parts of the National Park, giving a flavour of it all without embracing anything too demanding.

Scholars tell us that this wild, rugged region has long been known as 'Eryri', the land of eagles, based on the assumption that 'eryri' comes from 'eryr', meaning eagle. An alternative view suggests that it is derived from 'eira', meaning the land of snow. The truth is, no one knows, but the author takes the view that there is excellent foundation for supporting the notion that the lands of Snowdonia are named after the presence of eagles. This is a much more ideological notion, since eagles were once here all year round, while snow most certainly was not.

More than 25,000 people live within the National Park, of whom over 60% speak Welsh, and such is the popularity of the Park that it attracts over six million visitors each year. Most of the land is either open moorland, commercial forest or mountainous, but there remains a significant amount of agricultural activity. Since the local government re-organisation of 1998, the Park lies partly in the county of Gwynedd, and partly in the county borough of Conwy, and is governed by the Snowdonia National Park Authority.

Plaque, Snowdon summit

Anyone venturing into the generous bosom of Snowdonia soon finds themself in a landscape that has a marked and geological affinity with higher ranges elsewhere in Britain. And although much of the countryside in the valleys is beautiful, fecund and green, the terrain above the intake walls is invariably rugged and broken, a place where rocks predominate and the level of difficulty begins quite a few notches higher than a pastoral walk in Oxfordshire or the Chiltern Hills.

It is in the north that the principal high mountains cluster – the Snowdon massif, the Glyders (Glyderau) and the Carneddau, flanked by smaller groups like those of Eifionydd, embracing the

Nantlle ridge and Moel Hebog, and the much-quarried Moelwynion farther to the south. Within the scope of this book of short walks, many of the higher summits are unattainable, but they are there, waiting, beckoning like impatient children.

For the most parts, the walks in this book are low level, but there are a few high-level skirmishes, too, proving the point that here there really is something for everyone, from charming green valleys and mature woodlands to craggy topknots and fast-flowing rivers. There is, too, a rich and wonderful legacy of an industrial past from lead mines to gold mines and slate quarries, and a history of evil spirits and troubled times to rival any part of Britain. And if you're looking for film locations for television or the cinema, Snowdon has those, too.

But above all, this is a place to be respected and admired, not feared. A landscape to be loved, enjoyed and shared. This is a place where you can learn and hone your hill-walking and map-reading craft, and discover what it is that appeals to so many regular walkers not only in Wales but throughout Britain.

This book includes a list of waypoints alongside the description of the walk, so that you can enjoy the full benefits of gps should you wish to.

For more information on using your gps, read the *Pathfinder® Guide GPS for Walkers*, by gps teacher and navigation trainer, Clive Thomas (ISBN 978-0-7117-4445-5).

For essential information on map reading and basic navigation, read the *Pathfinder® Guide Map Reading Skills* by outdoor writer, Terry Marsh (ISBN 978-0-7117-4978-8). Both titles are available in bookshops or can be ordered online at www.totalwalking.co.uk

Llyn Geirionydd

- Woodland wildlife
- waterfowl
- monument
- lakeside path

walk 1

This straightforward and tranquil walk is of no little importance to those who study the history of Welsh poetry. Gwydyr Forest is massive (20,000 acres) and comprises huge stands of Sitka spruce, Japanese larch, lodgepole pine and Douglas fir. It covers a vast area of lead mining, which still has dangerous shafts, so it is important not to stray from the paths.

Memorial cross, Llyn Geirionydd

walk 1

START Trefriw

DISTANCE 2 miles (3.2km)

TIME 1 hour

PARKING Car park at Llyn Geirionydd (Pay and Display)

ROUTE FEATURES Woodland; lakeside path has slippery tree roots and rocks and *care is required*

GPS WAYPOINTS
SH 763 604
A SH 759 603

PUBLIC TRANSPORT None

REFRESHMENTS None

PUBLIC TOILETS At start

PLAY AREA None

ORDNANCE SURVEY MAPS Explorer OL17 (Snowdon - Conwy Valley), Landranger 115 (Snowdon)

Leave the car park and turn left along the road, but take the first turning on the right, at a barrier, onto a broad track (waymarked). The path touches upon the end of the lake, an area favoured in springtime by marsh marigold, lady's smock and bog myrtle, the latter, if crushed and rubbed onto the skin is an effective deterrent to summertime midges.

As the track bends left A near a stone cottage, leave it by turning right over a step-stile, to gain a path that sets off for the lakeshore, passing first across a cleared pasture before running below lakeside woodland.

The Forestry Commission's work at **Llyn Geirionydd** began in 1929 and now imbues the place with an air of tranquility, softening the effects of the intensive mining of the 1870s. The waste tip on which the car park stands and the adjacent mine levels were part of the New Pandora mine complex. Lead ore was delivered by tramway along the eastern shore of the lake, then by aerial ropeway to the Klondike lead mill and mine 200ft below.

Take care passing along the lakeside path as you cross slippery tree roots and rocks, but keep an eye open for common sandpipers and the occasional grey heron which favour this remote lake and rock habitat.

About two-thirds of the way down the lake the path seems to come to an abrupt end at a rocky point. But backtrack a few strides to find that it actually scrambles easily across a rocky shoulder, descending a little awkwardly on the other side to reach a fenced area of old mine workings. Here the path touches the lakeshore, before pressing on once more into the edge of the woodland.

The path eventually reaches a ladder-stile beyond which it keeps to the right of a low wall and leads up to a low building standing beside a rough track.

Off to the left is a monument topped by a cross, to which a short diversion is well worthwhile because it gives a lovely view back along the length of the lake.

Woodland path above Llyn Geirionydd

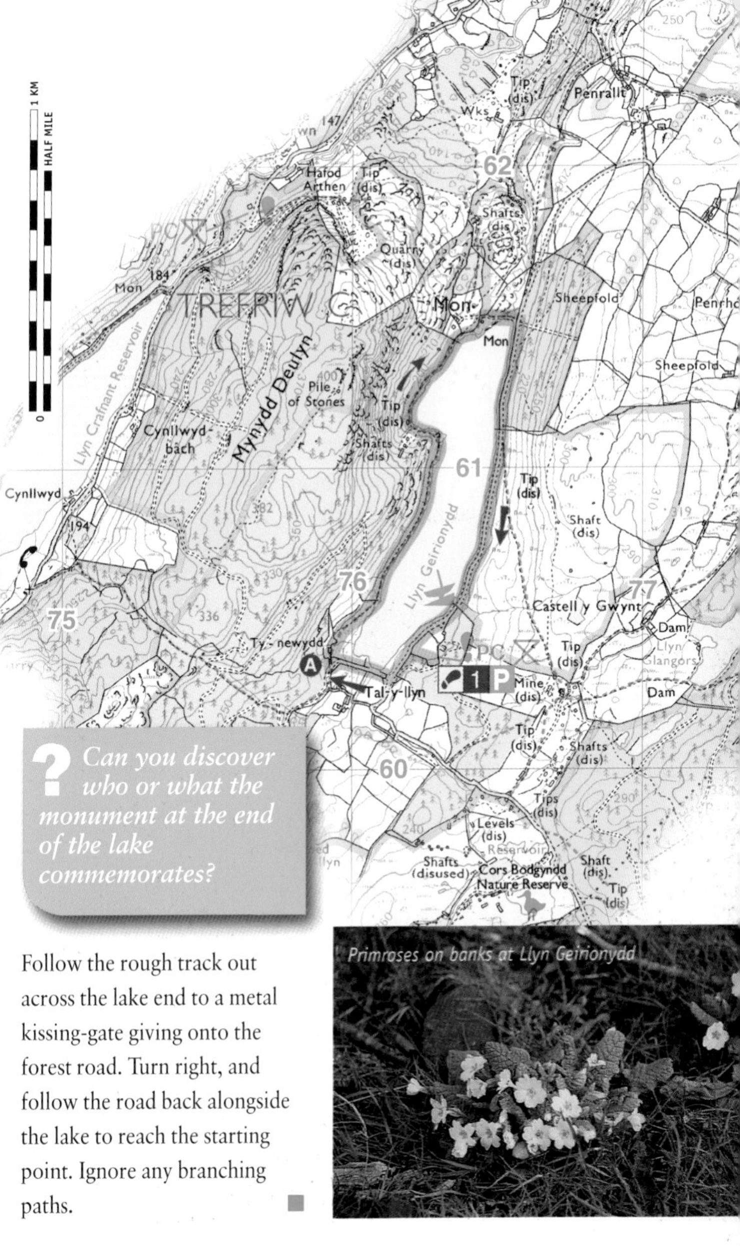

? *Can you discover who or what the monument at the end of the lake commemorates?*

Follow the rough track out across the lake end to a metal kissing-gate giving onto the forest road. Turn right, and follow the road back alongside the lake to reach the starting point. Ignore any branching paths.

Primroses on banks at Llyn Geirionydd

Llwybr Clywedog (Torrent Walk)

- Woodland trail
- White-water cascades
- wild flowers
- pleasant gated lane

walk 2

The 'torrent' in question is the Afon Clywedog, which here bullies a way through a narrow ravine, losing 300ft of height in the process. The result is a spectacularly turbulent river section that assaults eyes and ears as readily as the woodland garlic scents the springtime air.

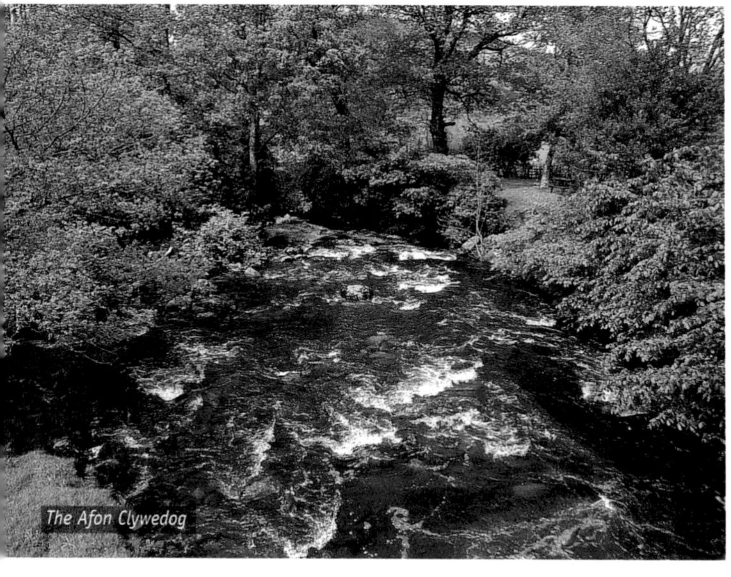

The Afon Clywedog

walk 2

START Brithdir

DISTANCE 2 miles (3.2km)

TIME 1 hour

PARKING Lay-by on B4416

ROUTE FEATURES Woodland trails; rocky steps; gated road

GPS WAYPOINTS
Start SH 761 181
A SH 752 187

PUBLIC TRANSPORT Buses along B4416

REFRESHMENTS Dolgellau

PUBLIC TOILETS None en route

PLAY AREA None

ORDNANCE SURVEY MAPS Explorer OL23 (Cadair Idris & Llyn Tegid), Landranger 124 (Porthmadog & Dolgellau)

From the roadside lay-by (not far from a school) walk south along the road for the short distance to a signposted path on the right.

Go through a gate and descend to cross a footbridge spanning the river. Beyond, a clear path leads downhill, never far from the turbulence. *But take care, the path has many rocky steps and these can be slippery when wet.*

The journey down to the foot of the torrent is delightful all the way, sheltered by mature beech trees, and offering many opportunities to view the torrent.

* The **Torrent Walk** was created by Thomas Payne who was commissioned by Baron Richards, Chief Baron of the Exchequer, to build an extension to the gardens of his mansion at Caerynwch. Originally, the path used both banks of the river, but one side has become overgrown and unsafe.

A Eventually the path leads out to a quiet road. Turn right, crossing a bridge, and almost immediately branch right onto a narrow, rising lane. A little more distant from the river, this nevertheless provides good views of it.

Steadily, the road (which is gated) climbs through pleasant woodland to meet the B4416, and here you turn right for the short walk back to the lay-by. ■

? ***The woodland area and the falls are popular with grey wagtails – a grey and yellow bird with a long tail which it wags incessantly. See if you can spot any.***

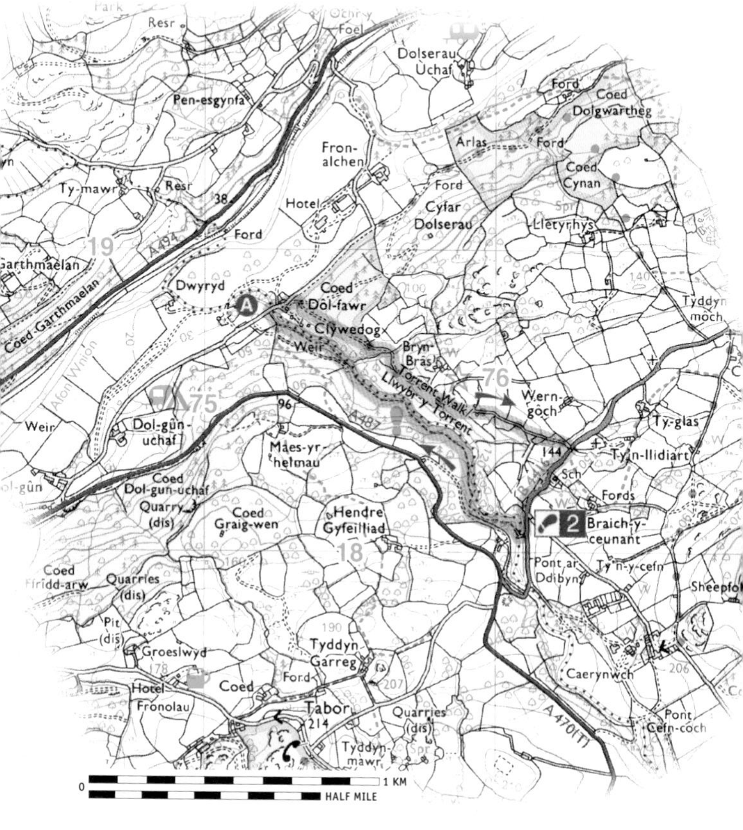

Afon Llugwy and the Miners' Bridge

- Odd shaped bridge
- woodland birdlife
- river gorge
- riverside picnic area

This simple walk is delightful, but you need to be careful about some of those steps because there are many slippery rocks and tree roots to contend with. *The Afon Llugwy ('afon' being the Welsh for 'river') is a busy river, bustling its way down from the mountains near Capel Curig, and barging through the narrow gorge which features at the turning point of this walk.*

walk 3

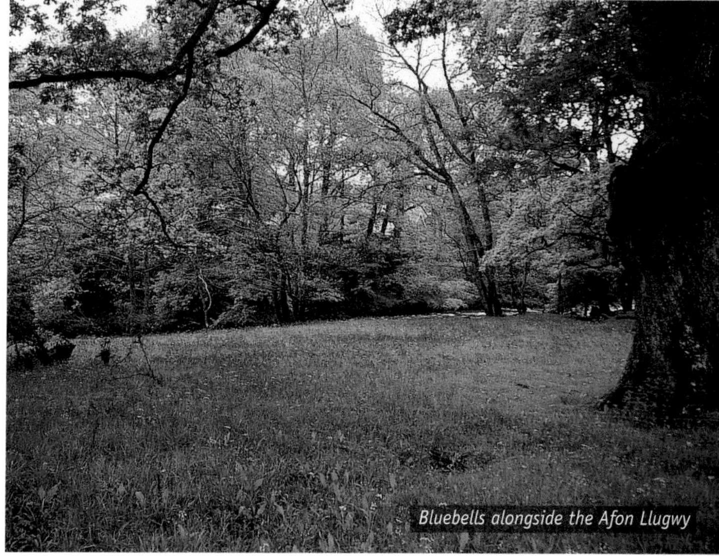

Bluebells alongside the Afon Llugwy

walk 3

START Betws-y-coed

DISTANCE 2¼ miles (3.8km)

TIME 1 hour

PARKING Car park at Betws station (Pay and Display)

ROUTE FEATURES Woodland trails and paths; riverside paths; forest road

GPS WAYPOINTS
SH 794 565
Ⓐ SH 791 566
Ⓑ SH 780 569

PUBLIC TRANSPORT Bus and rail services to Betws-y-coed

REFRESHMENTS Café at station and along A5

PUBLIC TOILETS At start and at Pont-y-pair

PLAY AREA Near start and at Pont-y-pair

ORDNANCE SURVEY MAPS Explorer OL17 (Snowdon - Conwy Valley), Landranger 115 (Snowdon)

Begin from the main car park in Betws-y-coed (though there is another near Pont-y-pair which can be used, shortening the walk a little) and walk towards the telephone box and toilets, there turning right onto a paved path across and then around a playing field.

When the path rejoins the main road, keep forward on a roadside path above the river. Keep an eye open for the darting flight of grey wagtails that love this habitat.

At the turning for Trefriw, Ⓐ leave the main road, crossing the bridge, with lovely views either side of the turbulent river. Take the first left after the bridge, and then almost immediately branch left, near a picnic area, onto a riverside path.

Head upstream, following the raised board-walk through mixed woodland of pine, hazel, oak, rhododendron and holly. In early summer the woodland is carpeted with bluebells, which bring an intense colour to the scene.

? *Can you discover in which year Dulwich College was evacuated to this area?*

Eventually the boardwalk comes to an end at a junction of paths and you must follow the

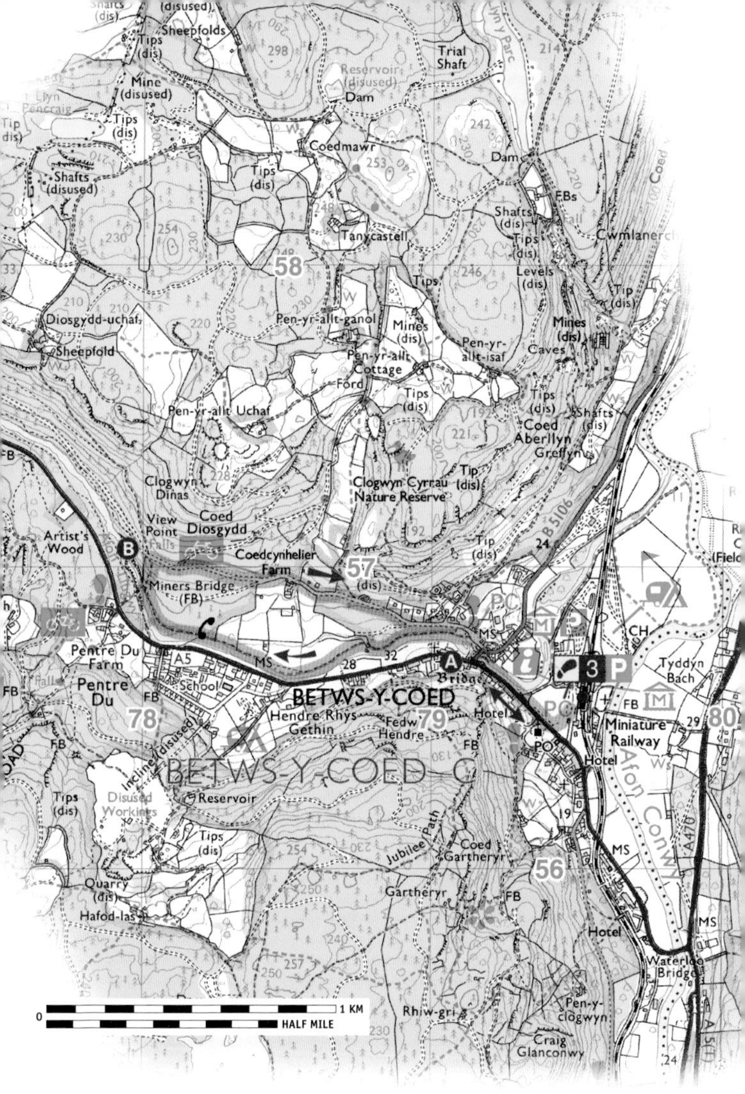

left-hand one, nearest to the river, which then leads around a rocky knoll to a ladder-stile near to the water's edge. Cross this and follow a clear footpath across a riverside field, bearing slightly right to reach another ladder-stile on the far side.

The Afon Llugwy at Betws-y-coed

Beyond the stile, you return to woodland, where the path shortly climbs a little to pass around an old mine, and soon arrives at the oddly shaped Miners' Bridge **B**.

Do not cross the bridge, but turn away, onto a path that climbs steeply but briefly into the woodland above the river. The path is not waymarked, but is clear as it ascends to meet a surfaced forest road.

> * The mines here were never massively productive, and are now all closed and lost in the undergrowth. **Miners' Bridge** was constructed to shorten the journey the miners had to make, and it provides a spectacular view of the river, as it forces a way through a narrow rocky gorge.

Turn right onto the road. When it forks, keep right, and follow the forest road back to Pont-y-pair and from there back to the start. ■

Llyn Barfog

- Enchanted lake
- superb views
- legends
- King Arthur

The fine ridge of hills north of the Dyfi conceal a beautiful lake nestling among the rock outcrops. Known as Llyn Barfog, which means 'the bearded lake', it is thought that the name comes from the lush growth of water lilies that spread across the surface of the lake during the summer months.

walk 4

Happy Valley

walk 4

START Minor road between Cwrt and Tywyn

DISTANCE 2 miles (3.2km)

TIME 1 hour

PARKING Car park in Happy Valley (National Park)

ROUTE FEATURES Farm tracks; upland paths; stiles; old mine workings

GPS WAYPOINTS
SN 640 986
Ⓐ SN 653 986
Ⓑ SN 652 983
Ⓒ SN 644 979

PUBLIC TRANSPORT None

REFRESHMENTS None

PUBLIC TOILETS None en route

PLAY AREA None

ORDNANCE SURVEY MAPS Explorer OL23 (Cadair Idris & Llyn Tegid), Landranger 135 (Aberystwyth & Machynlleth)

The walk begins at a National Park car park in the appropriately named Happy Valley, a dale of verdant beauty. Walk to the far end of the car park and go through a metal kissing-gate onto a farm track. Turn left towards the farm.

> * **Happy Valley** has long been popular with tourists since the railways brought Victorian holidaymakers to the resorts of Aberdyfi. It was at this time that the name 'Happy Valley' supplanted the original Cwm Dyffryn.

On reaching the farmhouse (Tyddyn-y-briddell), go left on a broad track to a high ladder-stile and then continue with the on-going track, which shortly starts to climb energetically.

Continue over another stile and climb on the broad main track, keeping right at a fork. At the next fork, keep right again, now on a

Llyn Barfog ('the bearded lake')

rougher stony track, and as this swings left, keep right again to follow a grassy track to a gate and stile. Cross this and drop to the shores of Llyn Barfog, nestling neatly in a craggy hollow **A**.

The path continues past the lake, but this is not your direction, though a walk down to the shores of the lake is quite in order. A short distance after

> * According to legend, fairies used to pasture their cattle around **Llyn Barfog**. A farmer who contrived to capture one of their cows was blessed with good fortune until in time the cow was sent for slaughter. As the butcher's knife fell, a fairy called the cow home: the cow, its calves and the fairy all vanished, along with the farmer's luck.

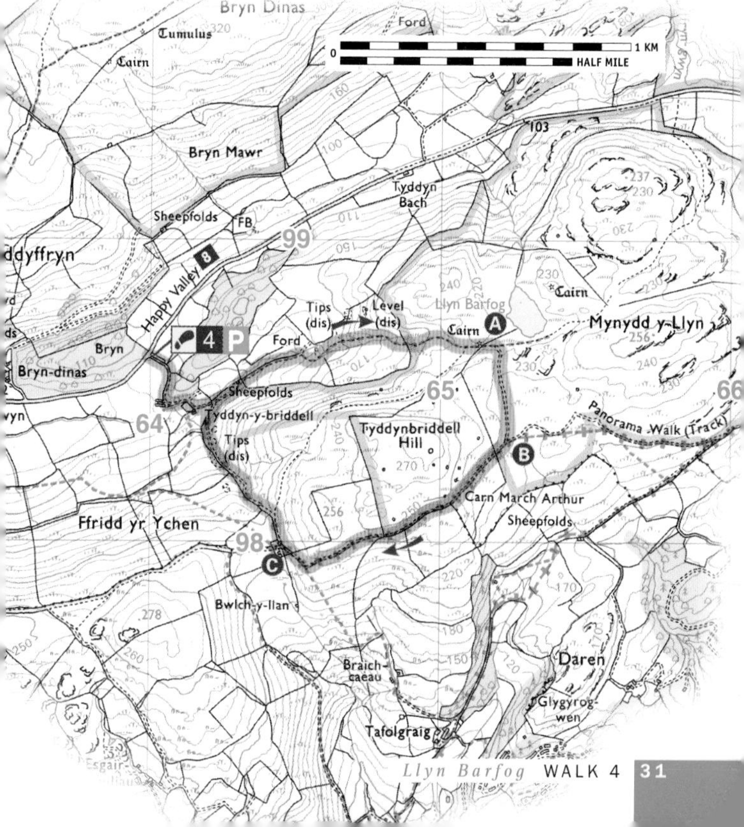

the gate you will see a gap on the right passing through the low ridge of hills. This is the way to go, following a path that soon widens into a grassy track and runs on to meet another **B** as the Dyfi Estuary and the hills of northern Ceredigion come into view.

Bear right to a stile and continue on the track beyond, following it in delightfully airy fashion as it skims along a hill shoulder and, after another stile, bears right to descend to an isolated cottage **C**.

Keep to the right of the cottage (ignoring all other signposted routes), and then follow a rough track that soon begins to descend very steeply.

Please note: *Young children should be closely supervised here not only because of the gradient but also because the area is one where lead was mined and there are still some open shafts to be found.*

Carn March Arthur

Follow the track down to rejoin the outward route near Tyddyn-y-briddell Farm. There, turn left over a ladder-stile to pass the farm and retrace your steps to the car park. ■

? *Can you find the hoofprint of King Arthur's horse?*

Castell y Bere

- Ancient castle
- attractive church
- Mary Jones' home
- beautiful valley

Set in a beautiful and fertile valley, this easy walk is both delightful and full of interest. The main focal point is Castell y Bere, stronghold of the last native Welsh prince, but there is, also, a poignant tale of Christian endeavour.

St Michael's Church, Llanfihangel

walk 5

START Llanfihangel-y-pennant

DISTANCE 2 miles (3.2km)

TIME 1 hour

PARKING Castell y Bere

ROUTE FEATURES Field paths and tracks (very muddy); narrow lanes; stiles

GPS WAYPOINTS
Start SH 669 086
A SH 667 090
B SH 670 093
C SH 671 088

PUBLIC TRANSPORT Buses to Abergynolwyn

REFRESHMENTS Pubs in Abergynolwyn

PUBLIC TOILETS None en route

PLAY AREA None

ORDNANCE SURVEY MAPS Explorer OL23 (Cadair Idris & Llyn Tegid), Landranger 135 (Aberystwyth & Machynlleth)

There is a small car park at the entrance to Castell y Bere, and from it walk back along the road for about 300 yds, as far as a path signpost on the right. Cross a stile and go forward across the ensuing field, passing around the edge of Castell y Bere.

> * **Castell y Bere** is a native Welsh castle built in 1221 by Llywelyn the Great to secure the southern border of the mountainous stronghold of Gwynedd. From the castle, which is freely open to visitors and well worth a visit, there is a splendid view down the valley to Bird Rock (Craig yr Aderyn), once at the sea's edge and still a breeding ground for cormorants.

Once beyond the end of the rocky outcrop that supports the ancient castle, keep forward along a fenceline to a ladder-stile.

Over the stile, turn immediately right and follow a fenceline towards a farm. At the far end of the field, go through a gate onto a farm access track, and bear left through the farm.

Near the farmhouse **A**, turn left to follow a track through a pen at the side of a barn, and continue over a concrete bridge that spans the Afon Cadair.

After crossing, go through the gateway ahead and then turn right to walk alongside the

? When was the Bro Dysynny Map made?

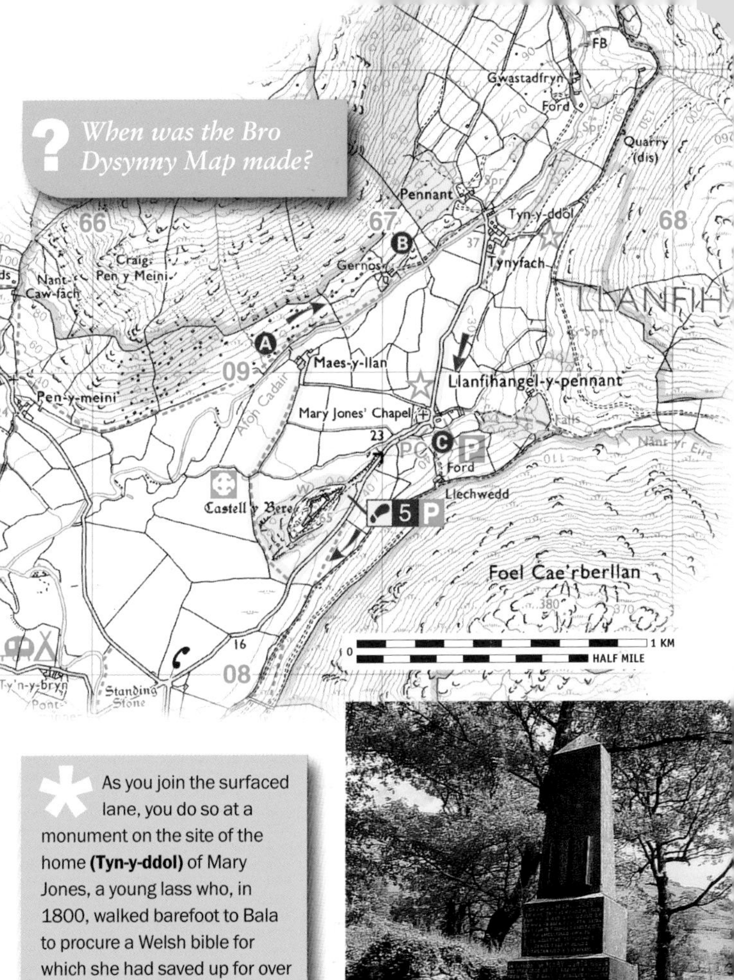

As you join the surfaced lane, you do so at a monument on the site of the home **(Tyn-y-ddol)** of Mary Jones, a young lass who, in 1800, walked barefoot to Bala to procure a Welsh bible for which she had saved up for over six years. Sadly, the Reverend Thomas Charles had sold the last bible, but he was so impressed with Mary's determination that he gave her his own, an event that was to inspire the formation of the British and Foreign Bible Society.

Monument Tyn-y-ddol

Cwm Pennant landscape

river with the fence to your right. Continue over a couple of ladder-stiles and some very wet ground.

At the second stile, turn onto a gravel track going past a cottage **B** and walk out to meet a surfaced lane.

Turn right and walk down the road to visit the church **C** at Llanfihangel-y-pennant.

Continue past the church and walk along the road to return to the start. ■

St Michael's Church is a 19th-century restoration of a much earlier church, probably 12th century. In the vestry is the full story of Mary Jones, and the Bro Dysynny Map. The Bro Dysynny Map is a three-dimensional model of the valley, (14 miles long and 4 miles wide), from the heights of Cadair Idris to Cardigan Bay. The details of the landscape are worked in embroidered fabric made by 18 people of all ages and both sexes, who live in the area.

Coed Ganllwyd

- Forest wildlife
- waterfalls
- gold mine
- picnic area

This brief walk from the village of Ganllwyd features some spectacular cascades and an impressive waterfall, all set in beautiful mixed woodland. Above it all, the lower slopes of Y Garn were a source of Welsh gold for many years, and the walk pays a visit to the remains of the mine buildings.

walk 6

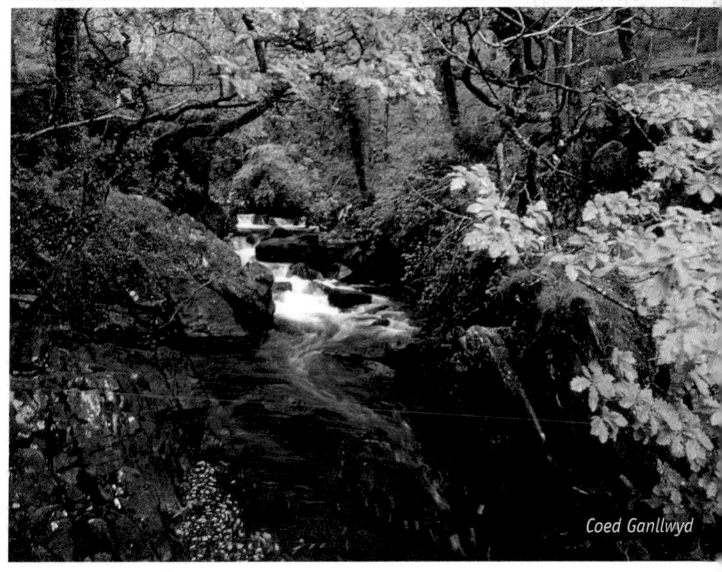

Coed Ganllwyd

walk 6

START Ganllwyd

DISTANCE $2\frac{1}{2}$ miles (4km)

TIME $1\frac{1}{2}$ hours

PARKING Car park at Ganllwyd

ROUTE FEATURES Woodland paths; upland trails; ladder-stiles; slippery rocks

GPS WAYPOINTS
- SH 726 243
- Ⓐ SH 722 244
- Ⓑ SH 720 240
- Ⓒ SH 718 234

PUBLIC TRANSPORT Buses to Ganllwyd

REFRESHMENTS Dolgellau

PUBLIC TOILETS At start

PLAY AREA None

ORDNANCE SURVEY MAPS Explorer OL18 (Harlech, Porthmadog & Bala), Landranger 124 (Porthmadog & Dolgellau)

Leave the car park and cross the road to a narrow lane (signposted to Rhaeadr Du) ascending through a gate alongside the Afon Camlan, which throughout its length provides exciting vistas of white-water cascades.

The lane is flanked by rowan, oak, hawthorn and beech, and when it forks, branch left, climbing steadily.

As the lane bears right, leave it by turning onto a rough path heading for a nearby waymark. From the waymark go left on a descending path to a footbridge spanning the river Ⓐ.

* Just before the bridge, high up on the right, is a slate tablet (erected in 1973 and now showing signs of weathering) containing a poem by **Thomas Gray** from his *Ode to the Deity of the Grande Chartreuse*. The original, now illegible and carved in an adjacent rock, is thought to have been done by the owner, W A Maddocks, of nearby Dolmelynllyn (now a hotel).

Cross the footbridge and turn right on a stony path *(very slippery underfoot)* that climbs to the spectacular double falls of Rhaeadr Du (*you will need to control young children here*).

The path climbs above the falls to a waymark, and here, turn left, up through the trees, soon to walk alongside a moss-covered wall.

Eventually, the path reaches another waymark close by a ladder-stile spanning a wall. Ignore the waymark and cross the stile **B**, then follow a narrow path through young, mixed woodland of birch, spruce and rhododendron with many of the trees encroaching onto the path and likely to give you a good soaking after rain.

> **?** *See if you can find a young 'Christmas' tree growing in the woodland.*

Continue to meet a broad forest track. Cross the track, and keep forward once more on a waymarked path of gravel ascending through pine trees.

The path presses on beside a low, moss-covered wall and a stream, and shortly touches on a major forest track at a bend. Ignore the trail, but keep ahead onto a way-marked track. A short way farther on leave the

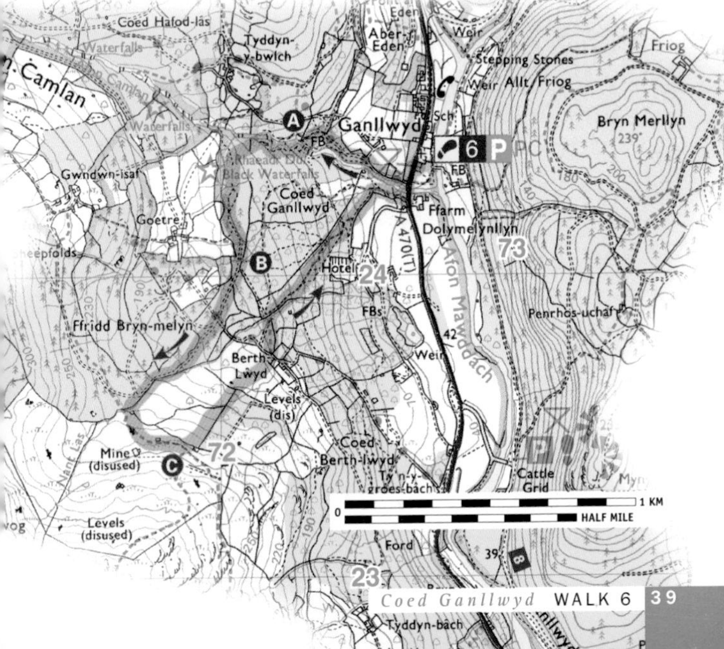

track at a waymarked stile of curious construction. Cross the ensuing wooden bridge and bear right on a 'stepping stone' path to reach a higher track near old mine buildings.

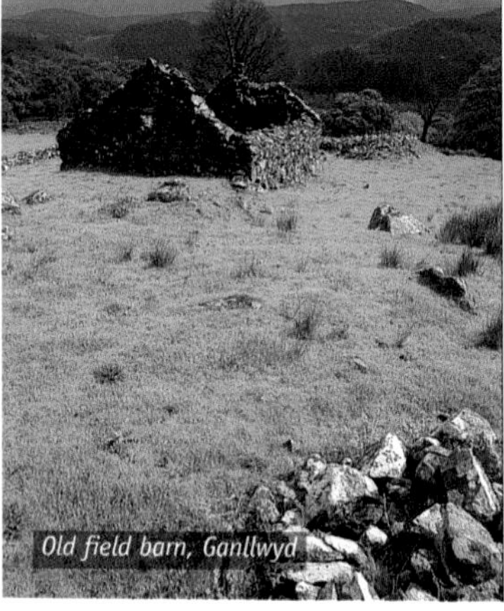
Old field barn, Ganllwyd

Turn left and pass the dilapidated barracks where the miners lived, and soon reach a high (and rickety) ladder-stile crossing a wall **C**. Over this, go down a grassy path through bracken (taking care if the grass is wet) following a waymarked route.

Shortly, pass through a dilapidated wall and head (boggily) for another ladder-stile. Over the stile, cross a stream and go towards a ruined barn, keeping to the left of it and descending to reach a step-stile near a gate.

> * The derelict mine buildings are all that remain of the **Cefn Coch Mine,** one of the richest and most extensive in Wales, stretching almost the length of the Mawddach Estuary. The Cefn Coch Mine was at its most productive between 1862 and 1914.

Cross a narrow surfaced lane, and head down a track to a footbridge and gate. Through the gate, turn right, descending initially beside a wall (and ignoring a path going left). Keep descending through agreeable woodland until the path reaches a low waymark near a fence and gate. Go forward through the gate, still descending, with the path soon running alongside the wall.

When the wall changes direction, go half-right to a stile, now with the Afon Camlan on your left. Continue down through the field and pass through a gateway to drop to the road near a house. Turn left to return to the start a short distance away.

Aber Falls

- Varied birdlife
- Welsh tyddyn
- spectacular waterfalls
- lovely nature reserve

The Aber Falls (Rhaeadr-fawr) has long been a popular walk with visitors to North Wales. In recent years the path to the falls has been hugely improved and is now an easy walk. This route, however, makes an alternative approach through a pine plantation before returning along the main valley route.

walk 7

The main track to Aber Falls

walk 7

START Bont Newydd, south of Abergwyngregyn

DISTANCE $2\frac{3}{4}$ miles (4.5km)

TIME $1\frac{1}{2}$–2 hours

PARKING Car park at Bont Newydd (Pay and Display)

ROUTE FEATURES Riverside paths; woodland trails; stiles

GPS WAYPOINTS
SH 662 720
Ⓐ SH 665 713

PUBLIC TRANSPORT Buses to Aber village

REFRESHMENTS Pub in Aber

PUBLIC TOILETS None en route

PLAY AREA None

ORDNANCE SURVEY MAPS Explorer OL17 (Snowdon - Conwy Valley), Landranger 115 (Snowdon)

Begin from the parking area near Bont Newydd, an attractive single-arch bridge spanning the Afon Rhaeadr-fawr (there is a Pay and Display car park over the bridge and a short way along the road. It isn't necessary to start and finish at Bont Newydd, but the riverside path makes it worthwhile to do so).

Aber, or to give it its full name **Abergwyngregyn** (the River Mouth of the White Shells), was the place where Llywelyn ap Iorwerth, called 'Llywelyn the Great', had a palace, a favourite spot with the Princes of Gwynedd.

Turn in through a gate beside the bridge and follow a lovely riverside path through woodland. Keep an eye open for dippers and grey wagtails, as well as buzzards overhead.

The path leads to a wooden footbridge spanning the river, beyond which it leads to a gate giving onto the main track up the valley. Turn right.

When the ongoing track forks, branch right. The track continues up the valley, but just before reaching a cottage, keep an eye open for a path branching on the left (signposted) and offering a way to the waterfalls through the valley plantation Ⓐ.

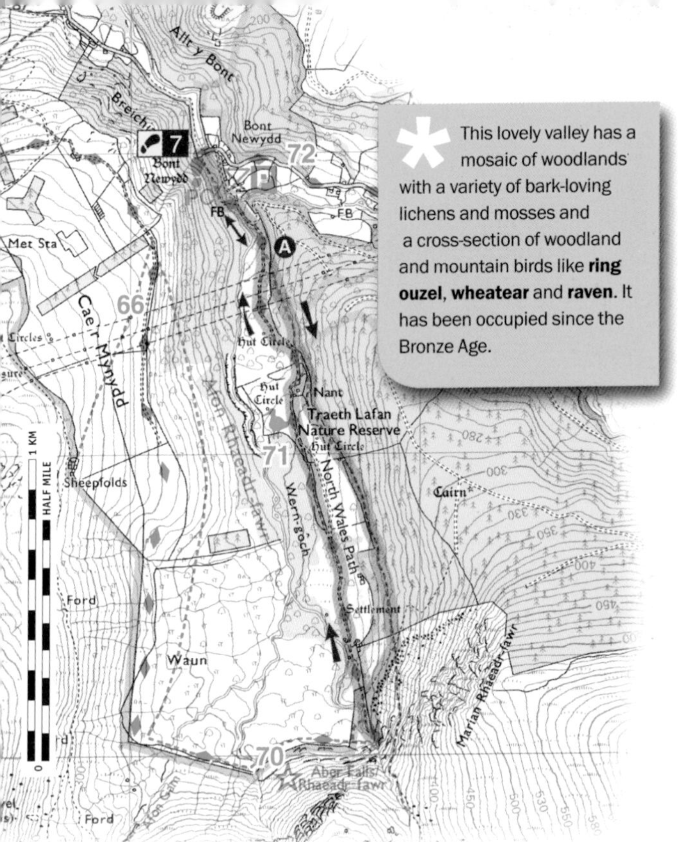

This lovely valley has a mosaic of woodlands with a variety of bark-loving lichens and mosses and a cross-section of woodland and mountain birds like **ring ouzel**, **wheatear** and **raven**. It has been occupied since the Bronze Age.

Initially, the path runs along the plantation edge, but at a stile enters the plantation. On the way, this route affords a lovely view of the Aber Falls and the slightly lesser falls (Rhaeadr-bach), to their right, both set in a wild cwm at the valley head, beyond which rise the domed and craggy summits of the northern Carneddau.

The path runs along an avenue of trees, mainly pine, all of which seem to lean rather drunkenly to the left.

At the end of the plantation, cross another ladder-stile and immediately bear right onto a descending path heading for the foot of the falls.

Aber Falls

The path leads down to yet another stile, beyond which the waterfalls, to the left, are easily reached. *Young children will need close supervision among the rocks at the base of the falls.*

Having visited the falls, and perhaps enjoyed a relaxing picnic, simply turn around and walk back out of the valley, following the main path.

Continue out of the valley, shortly rejoining the outward route which, just before a gate, bears left to cross the footbridge spanning the valley river and return through the woodland walked at the start of the walk.

* On the way out, the track passes **Nant Rhaeadr,** a typical Welsh *tyddyn* or smallholding, which kept a few cows, sheep and the occasional goat. The farmer used all the land available to him: the garden for herbs and vegetables, the mountain pastures for grazing, and the forest for firewood and making tools. Nant Rhaeadr was a popular spot with Victorian tourists, and was something of a wayside café, selling tea and home-made lemonade.

? *In the valley you will find some recording equipment. What is it recording?*

Bala Lake

- Glorious views
- waterfowl
- narrow gauge railway
- lakeshore picnic sites

This walk takes advantage of the narrow-gauge Bala Lake Railway that operates during summer months along the southern shore of Llyn Tegid. Using the train to reach Llangower and then walking back over the hillsides south of the lake, there are stunning views of the surrounding countryside and Bala's place in it.

walk 8

Bala Lake Railway

walk 8

START Llangower

DISTANCE 3½ miles (5.8km)

TIME 2 hours

PARKING Car park at Bala lakehead

ROUTE FEATURES Woodland trails; farm paths; roads

GPS WAYPOINTS
Start SH 902 321
A SH 908 320
B SH 913 325
C SH 922 333

PUBLIC TRANSPORT Buses to Bala and lake railway station

REFRESHMENTS Bala

PUBLIC TOILETS Bala and Llangower

PLAY AREA None

ORDNANCE SURVEY MAPS Explorer OL23 (Cadair Idris & Llyn Tegid), Landranger 125 (Bala & Lake Vyrnwy)

Begin from a car park on the northern shore of Bala Lake a short way north of the Llangower turning, and walk along the edge of the lake and over a lovely triple-arched bridge to reach the station. This top end of the lake has some fine willow scrub, popular with reed bunting and the rather noisy (but usually unseen) sedge warbler.

Take the train to Llangower, and leave the station there, turning left along the road towards the village with its pretty churchyard. Go past the churchyard, over a roadbridge, and continue to the next road turning on the right.

The trackbed of the **Bala Lake Railway** was once part of the old Great Western Railway line between Ruabon and Barmouth, closed in 1965 as uneconomical. Today's trains only operate between April and September, every day in July and August, but during other months excluding Mondays and Fridays. Information about train times is available by ringing 01678 540666 or connecting to www.bala-lake-railway.co.uk.

Climb steadily for about 400 yds, as far as a farm track doubling back on the left (footpath signpost) **A**. Turn

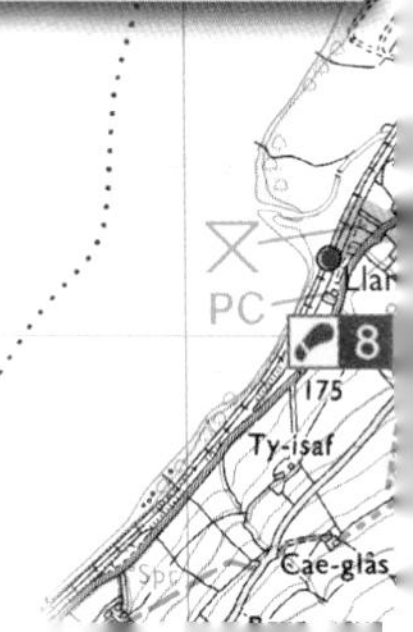

PC
8
175
Ty-isaf
Cae-glâs

onto this, climbing gently with a good view forward to the mountainous area north of Bala.

The track descends briefly to pass a farm and then climbs again. As the track bears left towards a large house, leave it at a signpost (waymark) going forward on a grassy track, passing to the right of the house, and then going through a gate on the other side. Beyond the gate, bear left to

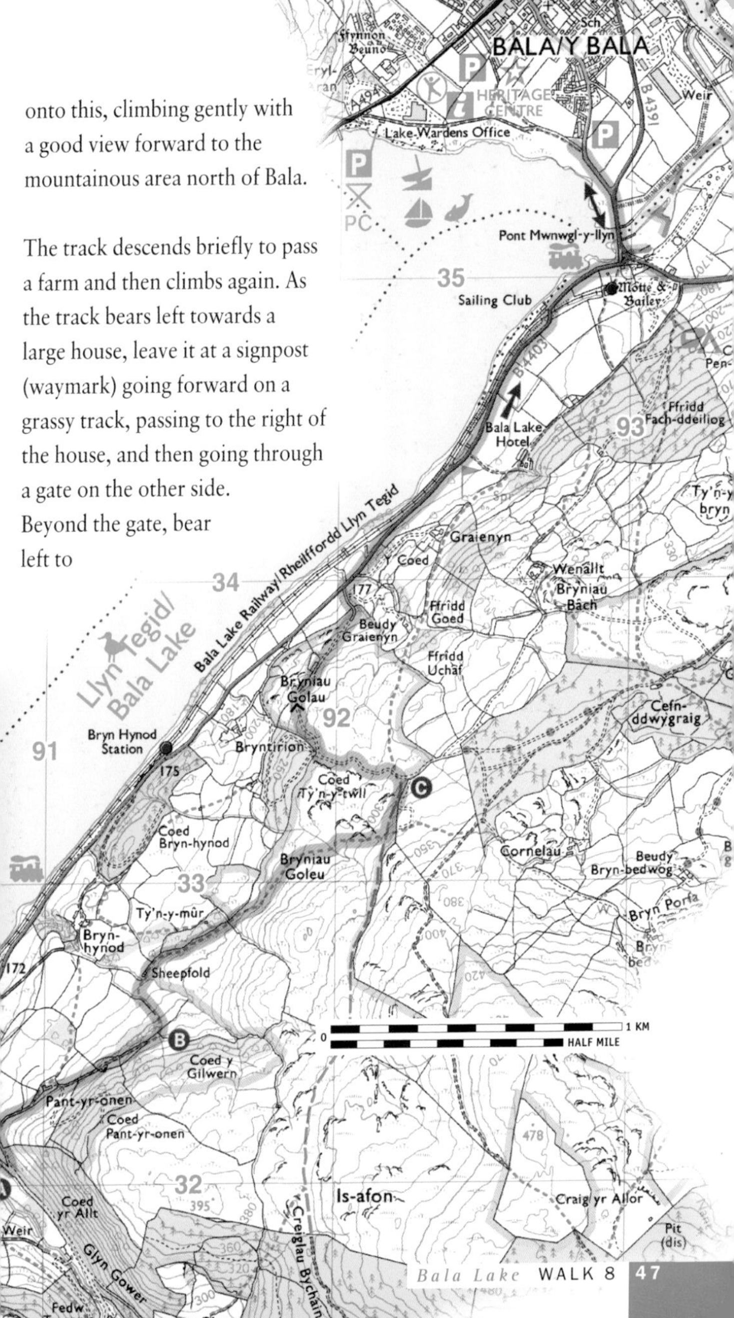

Churchyard, Llangower

another giving into the edge of woodland.

Now follow a path along the bottom edge of a wooded slope graced by some ancient beech trees. Part way along the slope, near what looks like an old quarry, go through a wooden gate and continue alongside a post and wire, with a lovely distant view of Bala at the head of the lake.

Once the highpoint of the path is reached, so the descent is leisurely, initially beside another fence.

A short way farther look for a waymark on a tree, at a stream crossing **B**. Here branch left, descending steeply beside the stream. There is no path here, and finding the ongoing route requires some careful observation, spotting yellow-topped posts. *Take care, too, on the descent, especially if the grass is wet.*

After about 150 yds, you need to cross the stream. Follow the posts to see exactly where to cross and then, once on the other side, bear diagonally downhill to a ladder-stile, the top of which you can see below, at the edge of another streambed.

Over the stile, cross a shallow ford and then another ladder-stile, continuing beyond alongside a fence marking the boundary of broad-leaved woodland. At the end of the woodland, the path forks. Take the right branch which climbs across a bracken slope, rising steadily as a grassy path to a ladder-stile on the skyline above.

Over this, turn left onto a descending bridleway, going down until you reach another stile. Cross this and walk down to intercept a surfaced lane **C**.

* In this wooded area, in spring and early summer you will find the lovely white flowers of wood sorrel, which favour the shaded habitat provided by trees and have leaves rather like **clover**. Keep a lookout for **bluebells**, too.

Now follow the lane down to meet the valley road, and there turn right, taking care against approaching traffic (the road is generally quiet but can be busy in summer months). If you timed your walk correctly you should be treated to a close-up view of the steam train. ■

? *In summer months the hill slopes are frequented by the white-rumped wheatear. See if you can spot any.*

Bala Lake

Cwm Idwal

- Mountain birdlife
- glacial lake
- rock climbers
- mountain scenery

walk 9

Cwm Idwal, popularly known as the Devil's Kitchen, is a ruggedly splendid introduction to mountain terrain. This walk, although rocky underfoot, is generally straightforward, but climbs on a stepped path through a massive downfall of boulders below the black gash of Twll Du in the valley headwall. This section can be intimidating and tiring, but is not unduly difficult.

Llyn Idwal and Pen yr Ole Wen

walk 9

START Ogwen

DISTANCE 3 miles (4.7km)

TIME 2 hours

PARKING Car park at start (Pay and Display)

ROUTE FEATURES Rough bouldery paths; rocky terrain; ladder-stiles

GPS WAYPOINTS

- SH 649 604
- Ⓐ SH 646 598
- Ⓑ SH 641 591
- Ⓒ SH 639 589

PUBLIC TRANSPORT Buses to start

REFRESHMENTS Snack bar at start

PUBLIC TOILETS At start

PLAY AREA None

ORDNANCE SURVEY MAPS Explorer OL17 (Snowdon - Conwy Valley), Landranger 115 (Snowdon)

Begin from the car park at Ogwen and walk around the buildings onto a rising, rocky path at the rear. This soon leads through a gate and over a footbridge spanning a tributary stream.

Follow the path until it reaches the shores of Llyn Idwal Ⓐ, a truly dramatic setting. Turn right to cross a double-gated footbridge, and continue on a rough stony path around the northern end of the lake.

When it becomes possible to do so, leave the main path and descend to a pebbly beach at the edge of the lake, and walk across to a gap in a wall.

> * **Cwm Idwal** and the adjacent mountains are designated as a National Nature Reserve for botanical and geological reasons. The landscape was shaped by glaciers during the last Ice Age, which ended about 11,000 years ago, and is regarded as one of the finest examples of glaciated landform in Britain.

Beyond the wall continue on a stony path through glacial moraine, heading towards the cliffs of the valley headwall, in which the black gash of Twll Du is prominent.

Beyond the end of the lake, a stepped rocky path Ⓑ begins to climb more steeply (the

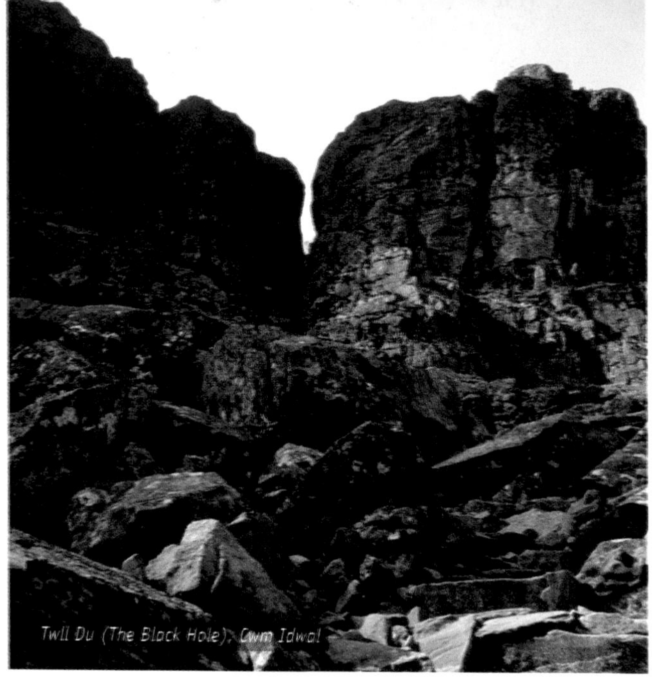
Twll Du (The Black Hole), Cwm Idwal

steps can be tiring). If the prospect of continuing does not appeal, simply turn around and retrace the outward route. Otherwise, ascend steadily, pausing frequently to take in the retrospective view of the cwm, beyond which the massive bulk of Pen yr Ole Wen looms impressively.

Higher up, the path threads a way through a massive downfall of boulders where, from time to time, hands may be needed to maintain balance: it's rather like ants climbing across a bowl of sugar lumps. *Young children will need close attention here.*

Eventually the path levels and passes a rough shelter beneath a boulder **C**. Here it meets the path coming down from Twll Du, also known as the Devil's Kitchen, and starts to descend

* Across this glacial landscape, vegetation includes **heather** and rare **arctic-alpine plants** and has evolved over the past 500 years as a result of upland farming. Please do not pick the plants.

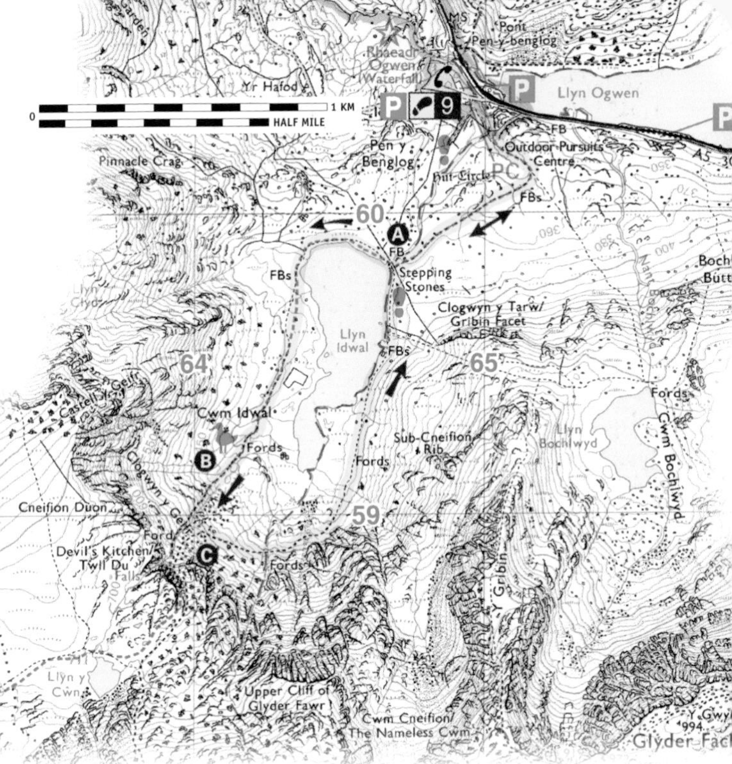

steeply. Follow the steps downwards, *taking great care.*

> ***?** The ring ouzel, also known as the mountain blackbird, looks like a blackbird, but has a white bib. See if you can spot any.*

The descending path soon breaks free of the boulders, and continues a constructed descent over an awkward stream crossing, *where again care must be taken* to the foot of a popular rock climbing cliff, the Idwal Slabs.

Continue past the Slabs, following a clear path out of the valley to rejoin the outward route near the gated footbridge. Turn right and return to Ogwen. ■

Llyn Elsi

- Mixed woodland
- mountain lake
- waterfowl
- forest wildlife

walk 10

This delightful forest walk climbs steadily to a tranquil lake set amid wild mountains. The route is straightforward throughout, but some care is needed towards the end as the path zigzags down through the forest. Keep eyes and ears open for woodland wildlife. Take a picnic to enjoy overlooking the lake.

Llyn Elsi

walk 10

START Betws-y-coed

DISTANCE 3 miles (4.7km)

TIME 2 hours

PARKING Car park at Betws station (Pay and Display)

ROUTE FEATURES Woodland trails and paths; lakeside paths

GPS WAYPOINTS
- SH 794 565
- A SH 792 556
- B SH 784 552
- C SH 789 558

PUBLIC TRANSPORT Bus and rail services to Betws-y-coed

REFRESHMENTS Café at station

PUBLIC TOILETS At start

PLAY AREA None

ORDNANCE SURVEY MAPS Explorer OL17 (Snowdon - Conwy Valley), Landranger 115 (Snowdon)

From the station walk out to the main road and cross at a pedestrian crossing. Turn towards the church, and take the first turning on the left, into a side street that leads round to the back of the church, from where a broad track (signposted to Llyn Elsi) sets off into the woodland.

The route, which ascends steadily, is waymarked by occasional wooden poles and leads through a beautiful mixed woodland of oak and sycamore, giving way higher up to various members of the 'pine' family.

Higher up, the track forks A. Take the right branch, and then pass other tracks on the left, right and left again before winding up to a T-junction. Here you turn left to emerge on the shores of the lovely Llyn Elsi, B surrounded by trees, but with distant views of Moel Siabod and the northern hills of Snowdonia.

Having reached the lake, turn right through a gap in some standing stones, onto a gravel path. This leads up to a memorial erected in commemoration of the opening of the 'Bettws y Coed Waterworks'. This is a splendid vantage point, and a nearby bench makes it a suitable place for a breather or a picnic.

Now walk past the memorial. There are three paths; take the middle one, which is narrow but well-surfaced, and follow it through some dense scrub, over a few boggy patches to a crossroads with a broad forest track. Keep straight ahead and follow the lovely trail down through the wood to join another broad forest track. This time turn right to follow the track uphill, but only as far as a crossroads **C**, where you turn left to drop back into the woodland on a steep and rocky path. This zigzags through the woodland, but finally emerges on the main track used on the

> * Keep an eye open on the way through the woodland for the moss-covered remains of a building on the left. These wooded hillsides would once have been populated, and the isolated buildings used for storage or for living in during the summer months.

> ? *The upper part of the plantation has numerous 'pine' trees. These produce seed heads, known as cones, but there are many different sizes. See how many different ones you can find.*

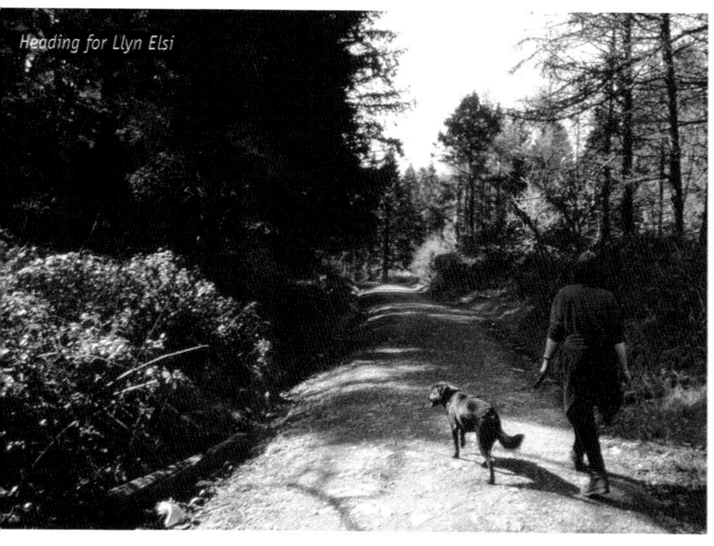
Heading for Llyn Elsi

ascent, near a signpost. Turn left and retrace the outward route to the start. ■

Monument, Llyn Elsi

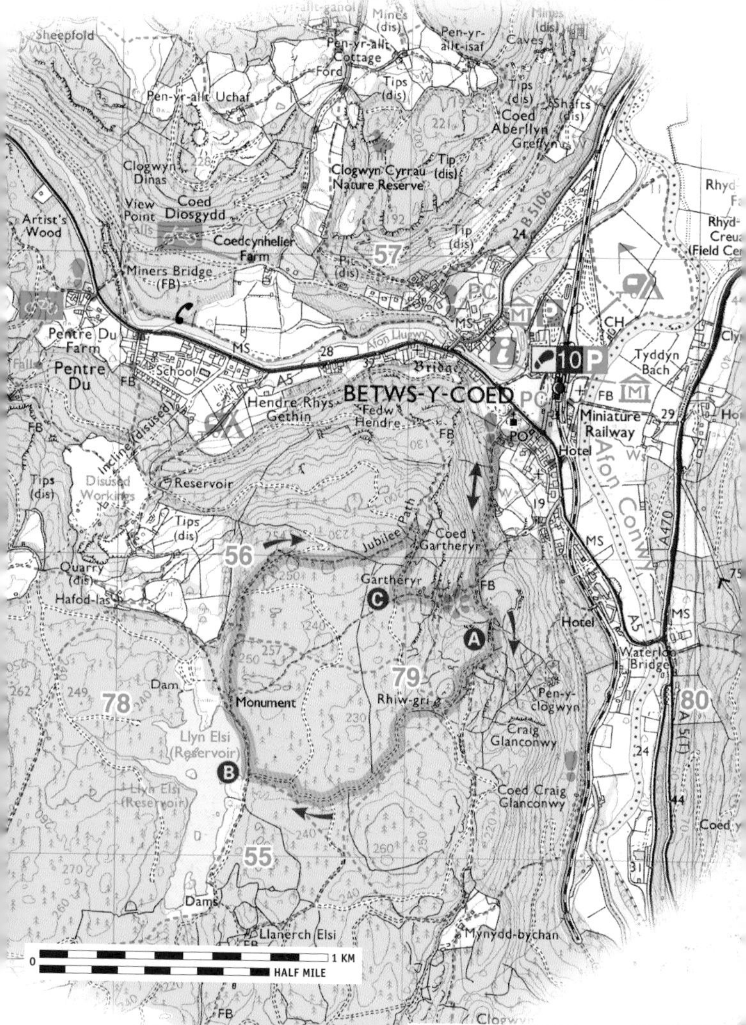

Sygun and Llyn Dinas

- Attractive village
- old copper mine
- mountain landscape
- excellent views

walk 11

This is a walk of two distinct halves: the first easy, the second much more demanding across mountain upland. Anyone reluctant to engage the climbs can simply return from Llyn Dinas. Two uphill sections are involved, along with one awkward moment at Bwlch-y-Sygyn, followed by some slithery downhill sections through rhododendron bushes. There are excellent views.

Beddgelert

walk 11

START Beddgelert

DISTANCE $3\frac{1}{2}$ miles (5.8km)

TIME 2–3 hours

PARKING Near Royal Goat Hotel (Pay and Display)

ROUTE FEATURES Riverside trails; mountain uplands; *two significant ascents*

GPS WAYPOINTS
SH 588 481
Ⓐ SH 604 488
Ⓑ SH 612 491
Ⓒ SH 606 482

PUBLIC TRANSPORT Buses to Beddgelert

REFRESHMENTS Pubs and cafés in Beddgelert

PUBLIC TOILETS In Beddgelert, alongside river

PLAY AREA None

ORDNANCE SURVEY MAPS Explorer OL17 (Snowdon - Conwy Valley), Landranger 115 (Snowdon)

Beginning from the car park near the Royal Goat Hotel, walk out to the road and turn left towards the bridge spanning the Afon Colwyn. Before the bridge, turn right onto a lane parallel with the river (signposted to Gelert's Grave).

At the gate that leads to Gelert's Grave, keep forward over Glaslyn Bridge, and on the other side bear left to pass the left-hand edge of a row of terrace cottages.

Cross a road near another bridge and go forward onto the Riverside Walk, passing through gates to enter an area heavily populated with rhododendron and gorse.

The riverside path ends at a ladder-stile giving onto a surfaced lane. Bear right, and at the end of the lane, go through a gate and towards the Sygun Copper Mine.

Continue as far as the entrance to the mine Ⓐ and there turn left onto a drive leading out towards the road. Go as far as a bridge spanning the river.

* The place by the river is the site of **'dressing' sheds** used as part of the copper mine. Dressing involved the separation of copper ore from waste by crushing the rock before sieving it in water.

Immediately before the bridge, bear right onto a signposted path heading up river. A delightful path now leads up towards Llyn Dinas.

* Beyond the river and across the road is a small hillock, **Dinas Emrys,** from which Llyn Dinas takes its name. This was a small fort, occupied during the Early Iron Age until the Dark Ages.

When the path reaches a footbridge, ignore it and keep forward to a kissing-gate giving onto the shores of Llyn Dinas, a lovely place for a picnic **B**. Here, through the gate, immediately turn right onto a clear ascending path up the hillside above.

At this point the nature of the walk changes and becomes more rugged. It is a good introduction to mountainous terrain, but not suitable for very young children as it involves a moment or two at the top of the second climb where hands (and bottoms) will be needed to aid progress. Anyone not happy with this prospect should simply retrace the outward route to Beddgelert and, perhaps, combine it with a visit to the copper mine.

The path climbs energetically for a while before finally taking leave of Llyn Dinas and looking forward as it crosses a stretch of mountain moorland where tough heather and bracken dominate the landscape.

A middle section that is level, leads to another uphill stretch, as the path climbs to a signposted junction **C**. Keep forward at this point (for Beddgelert) and

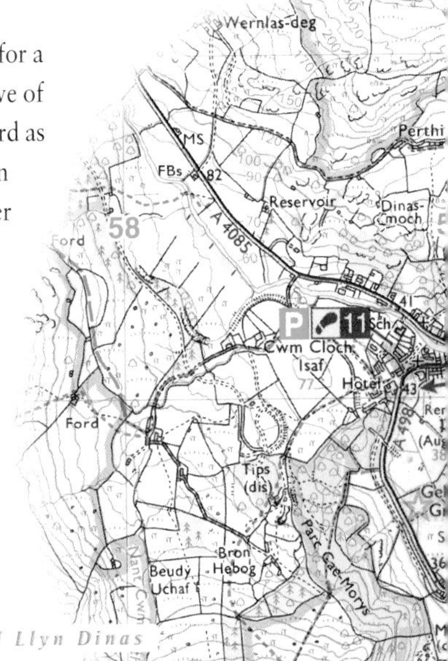

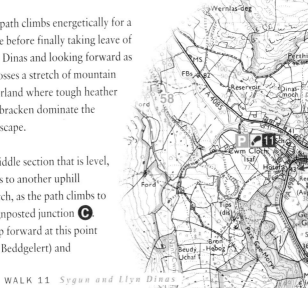

immediately pass through a small mining area with ruined buildings and mine entrances in the hillside that should not be explored.

> ? *See if you can discover where the Glaslyn Foundry is.*

Continue up to cross a ladder-stile at Bwlch-y-Sygyn, from where a fine viewpoint embraces Moel Hebog, Moel Lefn and Moel yr Ogof and the distant Nantlle Ridge.

Now, at the very start of the descent, comes an awkward moment as the path goes down a rock step. This is a brief interlude and easy enough to deal with (in reverse if necessary), but for a few moments it calls for increased care and attention. *Children will need careful supervision here.*

Heading for Llyn Dinas

The ongoing path soon becomes grassy, and just after it starts to descend again look for a branching path on the left, leading up to a signpost, and then continue for Beddgelert.

The path now follows the crest of a heathery ridge, with wild mountain moorland off to the left. Keep going as far as a large cairn on a rock outcrop, and here, at a path junction, bear right, descending.

More care is needed now throughout the remaining descent.

The path threads a way through stands of rhododendron, is rocky in places and elsewhere grassy. It leads to a metal kissing-gate in a wall, beyond which it continues as a grassy track.

In among the rhododendron the going is often muddy and slippery. Nor is the path as distinct as it might be and a bit of casting about may be necessary to find the driest line. All routes lead steadily downwards to the head of a lane that drops to meet the path used on the outward route. Turn left beside the river, and retrace the outward route to Beddgelert.

Llyn Gwernan

- Upland birdlife
- ancient road
- beautiful scenery
- wooded lakeside

This walk visits an area of Snowdonia better known for its high mountains than its peaceful tracks. But the walled track that is the middle part of the walk crosses delightful countryside with constantly changing views and a strange sense of remoteness.

walk **12**

Llyn Gwernan

walk 12

START Ty-nant, near Dolgellau

DISTANCE 3½ miles (5.6km)

TIME 2 hours

PARKING Car park at Ty-nant

ROUTE FEATURES Lakeside paths; ancient road; stiles; farm tracks; some uphill

GPS WAYPOINTS
- Start: SH 697 152
- A: SH 707 166
- B: SH 700 165
- C: SH 686 159

PUBLIC TRANSPORT Only to Dolgellau

REFRESHMENTS Gwernan Lake Hotel

PUBLIC TOILETS At start

PLAY AREA None

ORDNANCE SURVEY MAPS Explorer OL23 (Cadair Idris & Llyn Tegid), Landranger 124 (Porthmadog & Dolgellau)

From the car park, walk towards the toilets and go through a farm gate, bearing immediately right after a stream onto a broad track, but leaving it straight away to follow an indistinct path initially alongside the stream, then following a wall to two ladder-stiles, where you have a choice.

To follow the original footpath, cross the right-hand one and stay parallel with a wall, doing your best to avoid muddy ground and boulders – there is no distinct path here, but you can follow an intermittent line of waymark poles across a pasture.

> Behind you **Cadair Idris** and its acolytes loom large, filling the southern horizon. The distinctive feature of the range derives from the way ice has gouged great corrie basins into the volcanic rocks with impressive results, producing a huge scale of erosion that is in itself fascinating. For over 50 years, Robin Edwards of Dolgellau guided clients across these mountains, a practice that continued into the early 20th century.

On the far side of the field, the path improves for a while as it enters the next pasture, once more heading for a ladder-stile in a wall corner. Over the stile the path follows a boggy course through tussock grass and willow scrub, squelching finally to an end at another stile.

Beyond, more scrub awaits, but in summer the place is loud with the voices of warblers – wood and willow, chiffchaff and blackcap.

Ruin, Llyn Gwernan

The alternative route is a permissive path which avoids the worst of the boggy ground by crossing the left-hand of two stiles and following marker arrows around the top of the pastures. Both paths meet at the entrance to woodland just before Llyn Gwernan. Here, another stile gives onto a lovely lakeside path now followed leisurely.

Just as you are beginning to enjoy the lakeside path, it veers away into the cover of young woodland, and shortly heads into a pine plantation, from which it escapes at a ladder-stile giving onto a green track alongside a fence.

Go forward towards a ruined building **A**, and as you reach the ruin, turn left, and climb steeply on a grassy path, not initially very clear, but parallel with a wall. The path rises to a metal gate, from which it continues briefly along the boundary of mixed woodland.

Soon the path bears away and passes round (or over) a low hill to a stile beside a gate. Beyond this it encounters a stunning, enclosed ancient track **B**, probably an old drove road, that now strikes forward across an upland region that few (I suspect) visit.

? *Along the walled track only one tree appears. Can you discover what kind it is?*

With no opportunity to vary the route, the walled track heads roughly south-west for a mile, offering splendid views north to the Rhinogs and, later, south to Cadair Idris.

The walled path finally ends at a gate near a stone barn. Cross a small enclosure to a narrow metal gate, then look for a low waymark a short distance ahead, directing the path towards a wall, which it follows down to a grassy track where you should turn left.

Walled track above Llyn Gwernan

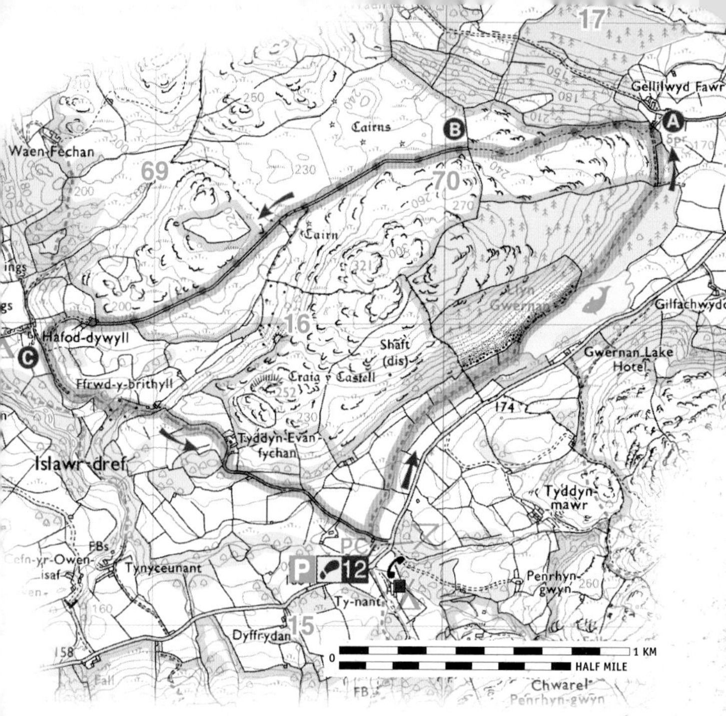

Now descend steeply on a farm vehicle track to intercept a wide bridleway **C**. Turn left (waymark on left), facing Cadair Idris. As the track starts to climb and bends left, leave it by walking to a nearby gate (waymark) beyond which the path descends gently into lovely birch woodland, which ends, all too soon, at another gate.

Through the gate, cross a stream and climb steeply right to a wide track above. Turn left, following the track, as, a short way on, it ascends to the right of a wall. Pass through a narrow section, beneath a strangely bent tree and turn right, away from the wall, to climb steeply to a waymark post and a gate.

Go through the gate, and go forward on a path enclosed between a wall and fence that leads to Tyddyn-Evan-fychan Farm. Go past the farm, and walk out along its access to return to the start ■

Coed-y-Brenin

- Woodland wildlife
- gold mine
- waterfalls
- forest trails

walk 13

This beautifully simple walk travels the two banks of the Afon Mawddach deep within the confines of the Coed-y-Brenin Forest. Always turbulent, the river produces an impressive display of force, as does its neighbour, the Afon Cain. Both meet up near the site of a gold mine, where the diligent and patient might still find a grain or two.

Afon Mawddach, Coed-y-Brenin

walk 13

START Ganllwyd

DISTANCE $3\frac{1}{2}$ miles (5.6km)

TIME 2 hours

PARKING Tyddyn Gwladys Picnic Site

ROUTE FEATURES Broad woodland tracks; footbridges; road walking

GPS WAYPOINTS
- SH 734 262
- Ⓐ SH 734 274
- Ⓑ SH 734 251

PUBLIC TRANSPORT Buses to Ganllwyd

REFRESHMENTS Dolgellau

PUBLIC TOILETS Ganllwyd

PLAY AREA None

ORDNANCE SURVEY MAPS Explorer OL18 (Harlech, Porthmadog & Bala), Landranger 124 (Porthmadog & Dolgellau)

Leave the picnic site by turning right onto the surfaced forest road, which soon degenerates into a stony track and leads past the holiday cottages at Ferndale.

Keep on above the narrow gorge containing the Afon Mawddach, passing a number of ruined buildings mostly associated with the lead and gold mines that once operated in this area.

Near the confluence of the Mawddach and the Cain Ⓐ, the track swings right over a bridge. From it a short path deviates left to view Pistyll Cain, a splendid waterfall tucked away in a corner.

Back on the main track, you soon reach the site of the Gwynfynydd Gold Mine Mill, of which only derelict buildings remain.

* Gold was first found in **Gwynfynydd** in 1863, but it was not until 1887 that the Welsh 'gold king', William Pritchard Morgan found the first major vein. The mine was closed in 1916, but in the 1930s there was an attempt to re-open the mine, and the mill was rebuilt. This was short-lived, as the mill burned down in 1935 before it became fully operational. The mine is now largely underground (for environmental and security reasons), and in recent years did start producing gold again, though this is now believed to have stopped.

The track climbs past the mill site and a short way on you need to branch right from it to reach a new footbridge, replacing a partially collapsed stone bridge seen just upstream.

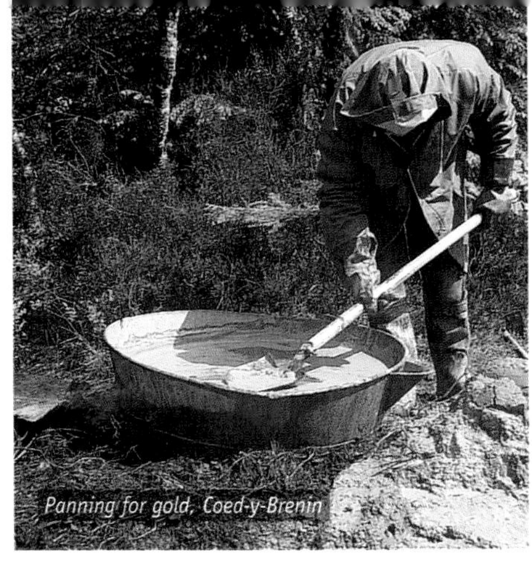
Panning for gold, Coed-y-Brenin

Over the bridge, turn right, climbing on a broad track, now going with the flow of the river. The track rises to meet another. Here, turn right, immediately descending.

Pistyll Cain, Coed-y-Brenin

When the descending track forks, keep right, always staying alongside the river.

Keep following the forest track for about 1½ miles until, just after a gate and a branching track (on the left) B, you can cross the river by another footbridge which offers a lovely view of the Mawddach in its rocky gorge.

Over the bridge go up to join the surfaced forest track and turn right, following this back to the start. On the way back, as throughout the walk, keep eyes and ears open for summertime warblers – wood, willow, chiffchaff and blackcap. ■

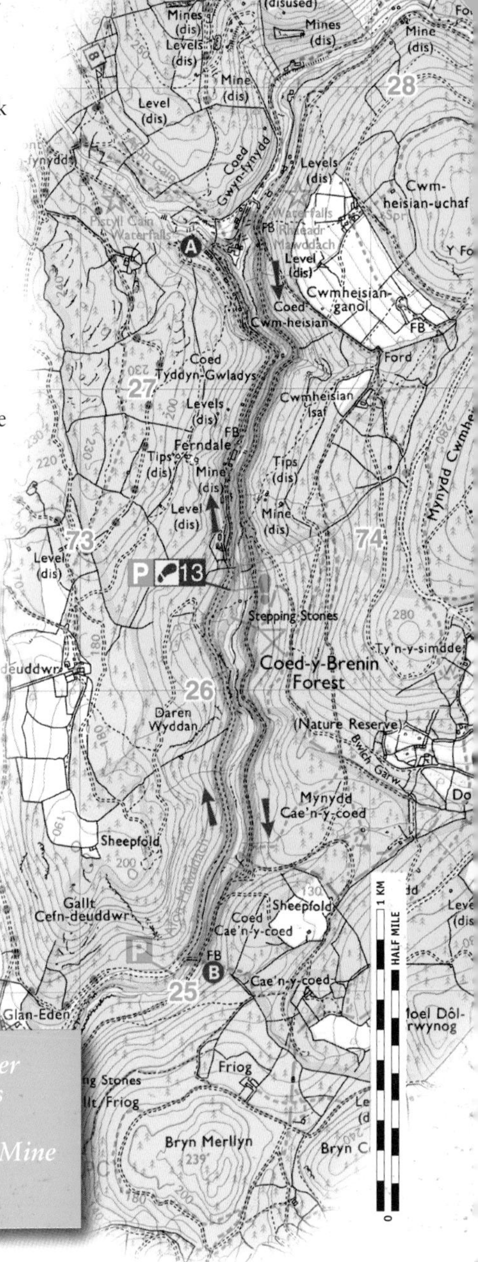

Above Penmaenmawr

- Upland flora
- prehistoric cairns
- stone circle
- wild ponies

walk **14**

At first glance the minor ridge sandwiched between Conwy Mountain and Tal y Fan seems innocuous enough, but it has considerable prehistory, in the form of hilltop cairns and stone circles, and an invigorating, airy feel about it – a fine walk high above the Conwy Valley.

Cromlech, above Penmaenmawr

walk 14

START Sychnant Pass, Conwy

DISTANCE 4 miles (6.5km)

TIME 2 hours

PARKING Sychnant Pass

ROUTE FEATURES Hill tracks and paths; ladder-stiles; vehicle tracks

GPS WAYPOINTS
Start: SH 749 770
A SH 747 761
B SH 740 749

PUBLIC TRANSPORT Bus and rail services to Conwy

REFRESHMENTS Pubs and cafés in Conwy and Dwygyfylchi

PUBLIC TOILETS None en route

PLAY AREA None

ORDNANCE SURVEY MAPS Explorer OL17 (Snowdon - Conwy Valley), Landranger 115 (Snowdon)

Begin from the parking area at the top of Sychnant Pass and cross the road to a gate opposite giving onto a broad path leading around a low rock outcrop.

After 200 yds turn sharply right at a waymark for the North Wales Path, onto a rising path. Using the waymarks as a guide, follow a twisting trail, mostly a grassy path through bracken and heather.

The Path, a moderate-distance walk across North Wales, climbs steadily, and when it forks, near overhead powerlines, keep left.

By continuing simply to follow the waymarked route, the path eventually meets up with the powerlines once more. Go beneath them and bear left, in due course reaching a ladder-stile beside a gate A.

Beyond the stile, descend a little across the western slopes of Maen Esgob, and, as you reach a junction of paths, in a shallow dipping valley, bear right, staying on the North Wales Path.

Huge standing stones dot this landscape, and many of the hills have large cairns on their summits, each with some past significance. Undoubtedly erected by man, they are a clear indication of the importance of this area in prehistoric times.

The path soon runs alongside a drystone wall, but then, at another waymark, starts to move away from the wall and passing beneath the powerlines once more, now going forward as a narrow path across a bracken slope.

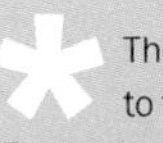

There is a splendid view westwards to the hills that rise above **Penmaenmawr,** many dotted with cairns, standing stones and more recent farmhouses. These coastal hills have been farmed for thousands of years, and continue to sustain a viable, if arduous, sheep farming economy.

When the path next forks, bear right towards a small stand of trees surrounding a derelict farmhouse **B**. Here, take your leave of the North Wales Path, by turning left alongside a wall.

At a nearby wall corner, keep ahead, walking away from the farmhouse, climbing gently.

The ongoing path maintains the same direction as it crosses the main thrust of the low ridge of hills, on the far side reaching a wall, now with a lovely view forward over the Conwy Valley.

Turn left alongside the wall, but later, as it changes direction, move away from the wall by following a broad green path. Before long, however, the path returns to parallel the wall and soon reaches an indistinct stone circle.

Stone circle, Cefn Llechen

Continue past the stone circle, beyond which the track once more temporarily abandons the wall and climbs to cross the shoulder of a low hill, later linking up with the wall again as the path starts to descend to meet a broad rutted vehicle track.

Follow the track, which comes down to a junction near sheep pens. Here, bear left on another vehicle track, but almost immediately branch left by turning onto a green path heading for a small lake.

Keep to the left of the lake, on a grassy path that pushes a way through bracken to a stile spanning a wall. Over this, follow a clear path, crossing another hill shoulder and then descending to a path junction.

Keep on in the same direction, roughly following the course of a wall, and shortly meeting up with the North Wales Path again, at a waymark, where the outward route is rejoined. Here, branch right and retrace the outward route to return to the top of Sychnant Pass. ■

This is a good place to keep an eye open in summer for the darting flight of **stonechats,** and for small groups of wild ponies that roam the hills.

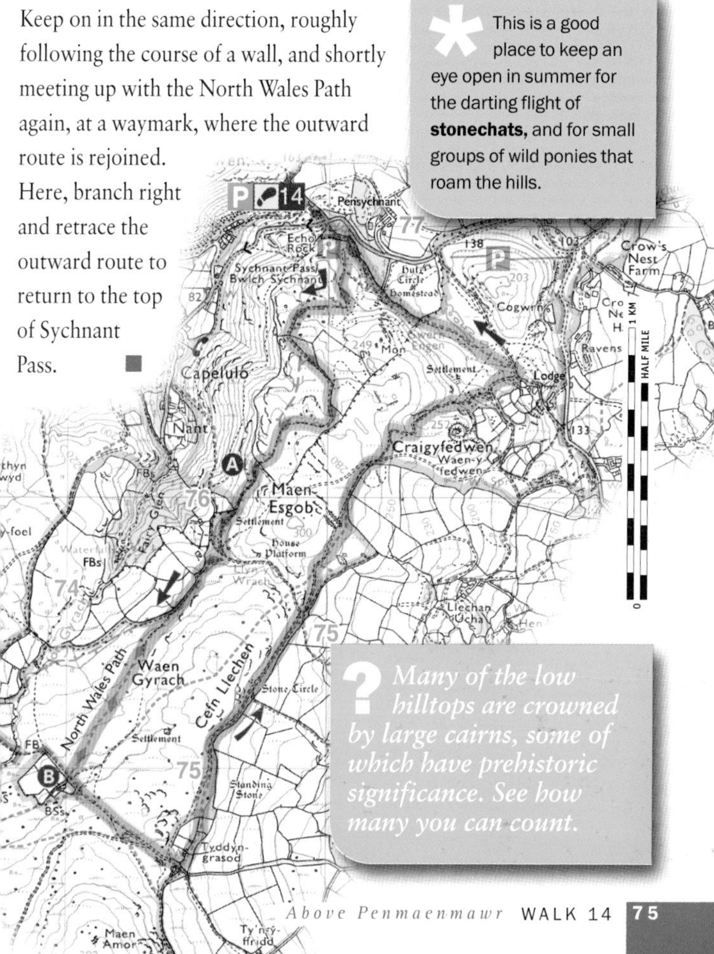

Many of the low hilltops are crowned by large cairns, some of which have prehistoric significance. See how many you can count.

Mawddach Estuary

- Estuarine birdlife
- railway trackbed
- woodland wildlife
- craggy upland

walk 15

Beginning along the shores of the Mawddach Estuary this walk later turns inland to an infrequently visited area of craggy uplands before threading a lovely way down through farmland and forest. The estuary is an excellent place to view waders and gulls, while the hillsides are popular with mountain birds like wheatear, pipits and the occasional ring ouzel.

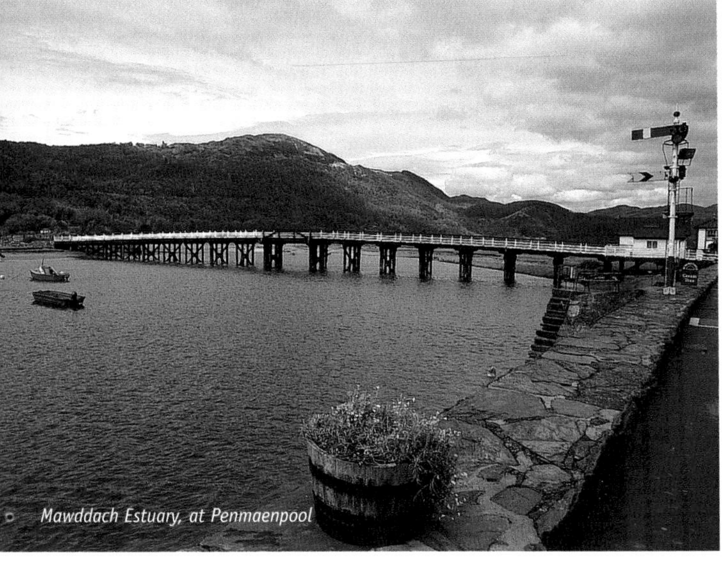

Mawddach Estuary, at Penmaenpool

walk 15

START Penmaenpool

DISTANCE 5 miles (8km)

TIME 2–3 hours

PARKING Penmaenpool

ROUTE FEATURES Estuary; woodland; mountain upland; farmland

GPS WAYPOINTS
- (start) SH 695 185
- A SH 670 175
- B SH 679 171
- C SH 689 174

PUBLIC TRANSPORT Buses to Penmaenpool

REFRESHMENTS Penmaenpool

PUBLIC TOILETS At start

PLAY AREA None

ORDNANCE SURVEY MAPS Explorer OL23 (Cadair Idris & Llyn Tegid), Landranger 124 (Porthmadog & Dolgellau)

Walk towards the toll bridge spanning the estuary, cross the road and go forward along the edge of the estuary, passing the George III Hotel. Initially, the track is surfaced, but it soon resorts to the old railway trackbed that ran from Barmouth to Ruabon, opened in 1865 by the Great Western Railway but closed 100 years later.

Go past cottages to a gate giving into a railway cutting, now regenerated with wild flowers, ferns, sycamore, oak and holly.

Keep going along the trackbed beside the estuary and eventually pass Abergwynant Woods on the left.

> * The **Abergwynant Woods** are one of only two surviving fragments of the woodlands on this side of the estuary that provided oak for the shipbuilding that took place in creeks along the river during the 18th and 19th centuries.

Gradually the trackbed closes in on the estuary until finally it is travelling alongside it, at the water's edge. Keep an eye open along this stretch for the large black and white shelduck, which has a broad chestnut band around its chest. The ducks are often found on the estuary in pairs or small groups.

Continue along the trackbed until you reach a bridge spanning the in-flowing Afon Gwynant **A**, and before you start to cross it, leave the trackbed by branching left onto a broad track alongside the river.

Follow the riverside track into woodland, and eventually turn right, through a metal gate (waymark) towards Abergwynant Farm. The track soon rejoins the company of the river, which is usually fast flowing, and leading out to a single-arched bridge near the farm.

Ignore the bridge, and go forward onto a surfaced farm access, which leads attractively up to a road junction. There turn left but immediately leave the road by branching right onto a side road leading to a youth hostel, initially climbing steeply through woodland.

Old railway station, Penmaenpool

Walk up the road, flanked by bluebells, celandine and Welsh poppies, and pass along the top edge of the river gorge, through which the Gwynant forces a white-water way. Continue as far as the turning to Cae'n-y-coed **B**. Here leave the ascending road and branch left through a metal gate.

When the ensuing farm access forks, branch right to a gate and stile. The ongoing track zigzags upwards and eventually climbs to run just below

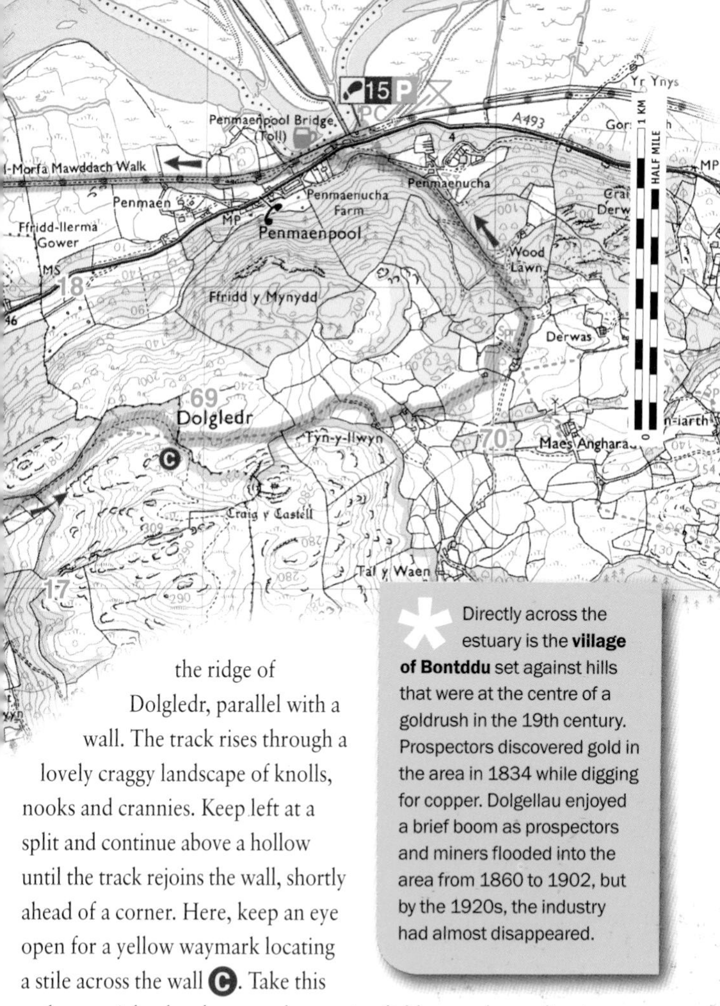

the ridge of Dolgledr, parallel with a wall. The track rises through a lovely craggy landscape of knolls, nooks and crannies. Keep left at a split and continue above a hollow until the track rejoins the wall, shortly ahead of a corner. Here, keep an eye open for a yellow waymark locating a stile across the wall **C**. Take this and go straight ahead, across the ensuing field, soon descending into a shallow valley, where you turn left.

A narrow path runs through the valley, eventually close by a fence leading down to a ladder-stile. Beyond, a green path accompanies a wall and then goes past a small copse before crossing a tumbledown wall and turning right to another stile.

Directly across the estuary is the **village of Bontddu** set against hills that were at the centre of a goldrush in the 19th century. Prospectors discovered gold in the area in 1834 while digging for copper. Dolgellau enjoyed a brief boom as prospectors and miners flooded into the area from 1860 to 1902, but by the 1920s, the industry had almost disappeared.

Mawddach woodland

From the stile bear left on a rough vehicle track. As you approach a corrugated iron-roofed stone barn in a wall corner, keep an eye open for a low waymark pole on the left with the number 7 on it, and from this strike down-field towards a farm.

Go through two gates and then take a track on the left to another ladder-stile and gate from which a rough track runs on. It climbs past a slate-roofed barn (now as a permissive path) and curves right before rejoining the right of way at a signpost.

Turn left onto a rough access track, but as this swings right, leave it by going left across a narrow grassy col between two low hills (waymark), and immediately locate a stile giving into cleared woodland.

A path leads down to meet a forest trail. Go left onto this and continue as far as the first cottage on the right. There turn through a narrow gate with a waymark on it. Turn through this and follow a path down to the Penmaenpool road.

At the road, cross with care, and then turn left down towards the George III Hotel, there rejoining the estuary path a short distance from the start. ■

? The Welsh gold found above the Mawddach Estuary is renowned for its light colour and was traditionally used for a special purpose. Can you discover what that purpose was?

Yr Wyddfa (Snowdon)

- Mountain railway
- stupendous views
- rugged scenery
- mountain summit

Although only taken in descent, this visit to the summit of England and Wales is still a tough walk and needs decent footwear and wind- and waterproof clothing. Best reserved for a clear day, *this walk provides superb views of the high mountains and Wales, and gives an invigorating sense of freedom.*

walk 16

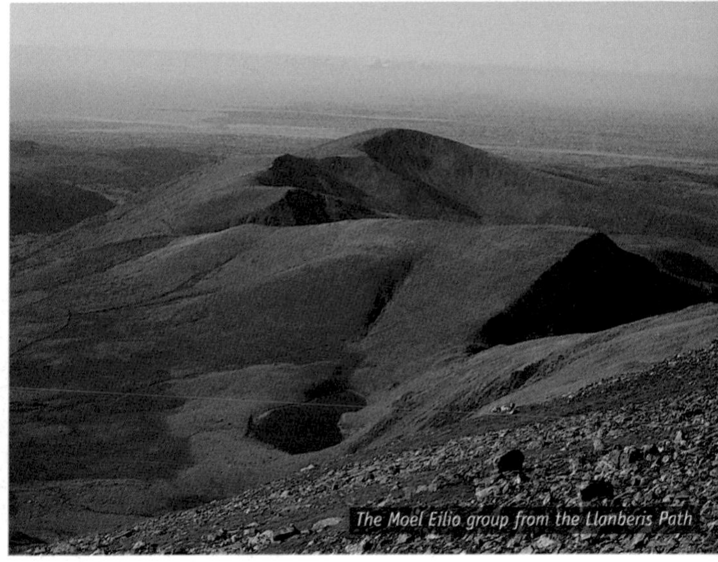

The Moel Eilio group from the Llanberis Path

walk 16

START Llanberis

DISTANCE $4\frac{3}{4}$ miles (7.5km)

TIME 2 hours

PARKING Llanberis

ROUTE FEATURES High mountain paths; steep slopes; loose stones

GPS WAYPOINTS
- SH 609 543
- Ⓐ SH 607 548
- Ⓑ SH 608 560
- Ⓒ SH 594 576

PUBLIC TRANSPORT Buses to Llanberis

REFRESHMENTS Llanberis and at Snowdon summit

PUBLIC TOILETS At start and Snowdon summit

PLAY AREA None

ORDNANCE SURVEY MAPS Explorer OL17 (Snowdon - Conwy Valley), Landranger 115 (Snowdon)

Take the mountain railway to the summit of Snowdon, enjoying the hour-long steady climb up to the top of the mountain. Once at the top, walk steeply up to the summit cairn and/or visit the new café building before setting off down.

The descending track initially is very close to the railway, and leads first to a large standing stone Ⓐ from which there is a stupendous view eastwards to Crib Goch, the Glyders, Moel Siabod and the three lakes visited in *Walk 19*.

Keep on past the standing stone, and soon the ongoing path forks. The right branch climbs onto the second highest summit hereabouts, Crib-y-ddysgl, but you should ignore this and keep forward, still following the course of the railway, though this is now dropping away from the path.

The path curves gently around the north-western shoulder of Crib-y-ddysgl and then starts to descend very steeply on loose stones and rocks. *Take great care here*.

Gradually, the path levels as it runs beside the railway again on the approach to Clogwyn Station. The path passes very close to the rim of Cwm Hetiau Ⓑ (*keep children under close control here*) before swinging left through a

The idea of a mountain railway on Snowdon was originated early in the 19th century, but it was only with the formation of the **Snowdon Mountain Tramroad and Hotels Company** in 1894 that the possibility came to fruition. There are nine operational locomotives today: five steam and four diesels. The average gradient is 1:7.8 (12.85%) and the steepest is 1:5.5 (18%).

tunnel beneath the railway.

Beyond the tunnel, keep forward, descending again, now mainly on recently constructed rocky

Y Lliwedd from the summit of Snowdon

steps. Off to the left you can see the stern dark cliffs of Clogwyn Du'r Arddu, one of the most severe climbing 'playgrounds' in Wales.

The path pulls away from the cliffs and continues down, passing the Halfway Café, where you can get refreshments, before crossing the track again **C**. The gradient is now much easier as the path continues its

Clogwyn Du'r Arddu was the scene during the 1950s and 1960s of many early rock-climbing routes, then at the highest extreme of climbing. Many were first ascended by the Salford pairing of Don Whillans and Joe Brown, but later climbers have added their own tally of impressive routes to the 'black cliff'. *This is not a place for novices.*

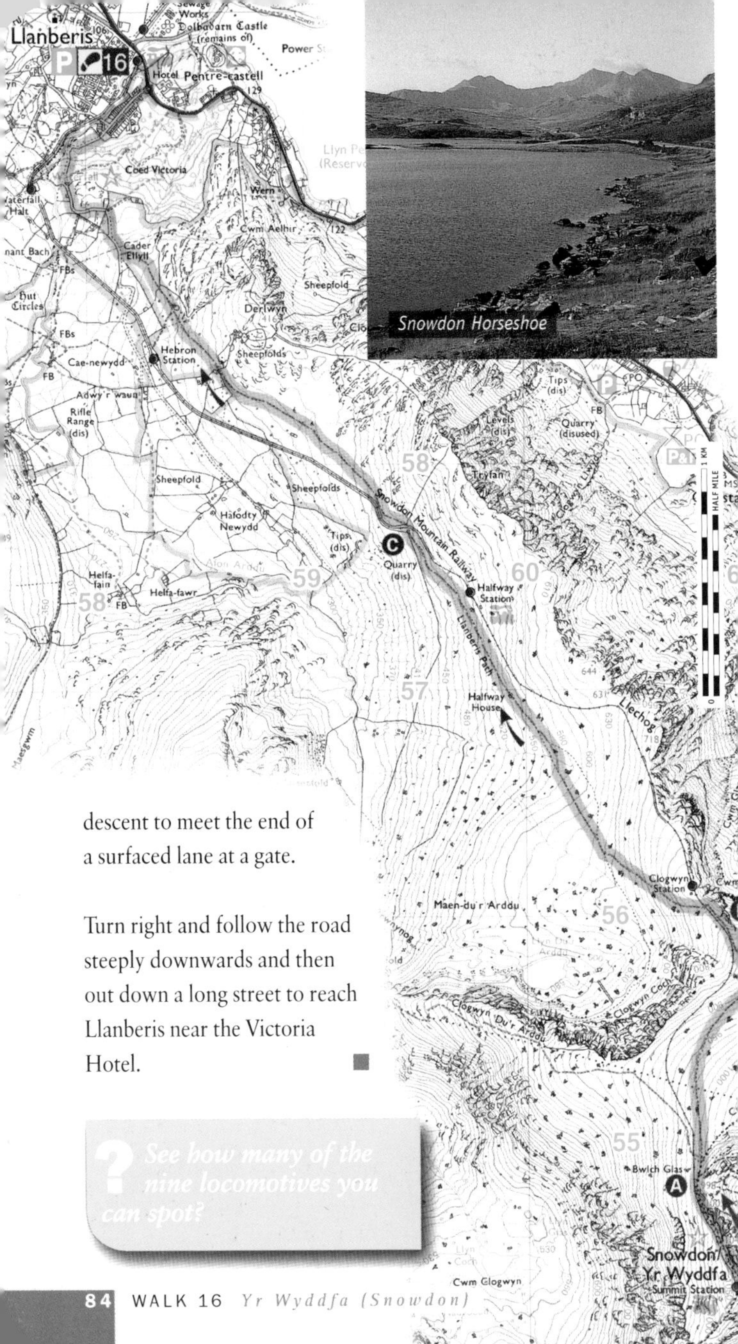

Snowdon Horseshoe

descent to meet the end of a surfaced lane at a gate.

Turn right and follow the road steeply downwards and then out down a long street to reach Llanberis near the Victoria Hotel. ■

See how many of the nine locomotives you can spot?

Cwm Bochlwyd and Cwm Tryfan

- Mountain birdlife
- cliffs and lakes
- high pass
- the Miners' Track

Offering the most demanding walk in the book, *this ascent to Cwm Bochlwyd across into the neighbouring Cwm Tryfan effectively circles the great peak, Tryfan, which towers above the A5 at Ogwen.* This is a rugged, enjoyable walk, requiring suitable footwear and wind/rainproof clothing – though it is best not tackled in such conditions. Take plenty of refreshments.

walk **17**

Cwm Bochlwyd

walk 17

START Ogwen

DISTANCE 4½ miles (7.3km)

HEIGHT GAIN 1,395ft (425m)

TIME 3 hours

PARKING Ogwen

ROUTE FEATURES Mountain paths and lakes; stream crossing, stiles; rough paths

GPS WAYPOINTS

- Start: SH 649 604
- Ⓐ SH 651 601
- Ⓑ SH 655 594
- Ⓒ SH 662 589
- Ⓓ SH 671 600

PUBLIC TRANSPORT Buses to Ogwen

REFRESHMENTS Ogwen

PUBLIC TOILETS At start

PLAY AREA None

ORDNANCE SURVEY MAPS Explorer OL17 (Snowdon - Conwy Valley), Landranger 115 (Snowdon)

Begin from the car park at Ogwen and walk around the buildings onto a rising, rocky path at the rear. This soon leads through a gate and over a footbridge spanning a tributary stream.

> ? *The most common bird along this walk is the meadow pipit: a small brown bird with white outer tail feathers. See if you can spot any.*

Continue with the path until it turns abruptly to the right to head for Cwm Idwal *(Walk 9)*. Here, on the apex of the bend leave the main track by turning onto a less distinct path Ⓐ tracking across upland pasture towards the conspicuous cliff, Bochlwyd Buttress (look for the elongated letter 'H' formed by cracks on its face).

As you near Bochlwyd Buttress the path begins to climb steeply. It has been improved in recent years and though steep is a sure and

> * **Cwm Bochlwyd** is a wonderful place to savour the mountain environment. Glyder Fach looms darkly above you, while shapely Tryfan stands off to the left, an enticing summit, but too complex for the purposes of this book. Within the cwm lies Llyn Bochlwyd, and many a backpacker has spent a peaceful night camped here.

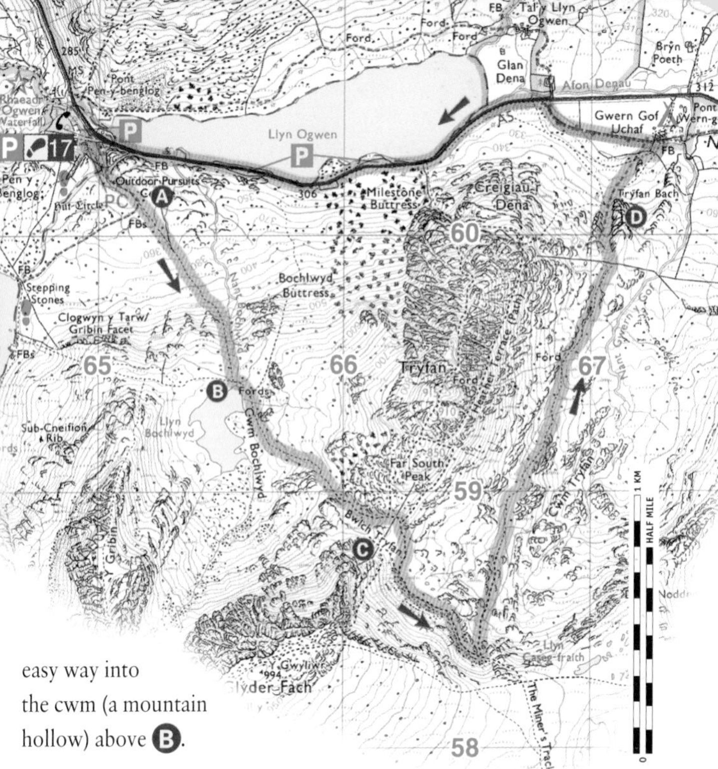

easy way into the cwm (a mountain hollow) above **B**.

With the lake to your right, you need to cross the outflowing stream, and then follow a clear rocky path that climbs steadily and steeply to a couple of ladder-stiles that appear on the skyline above. These mark Bwlch Tryfan **C**, a high mountain pass.

Over the stiles, keep forward, looking for a clear path descending into the great hollow that now appears ahead. This is Cwm Tryfan, and a good if rough path runs down its length. A couple of false starts do lead into the path, and it is a question

* The path up to and beyond **Bwlch Tryfan** is a section of **the Miners' Track**, which continues towards the mines below Snowdon. This is the way workers who lived in Bethesda would walk each week to and from their workplace on the other side of the mountain.

Falls near Ogwen

of taking the one you feel most comfortable with, although none is especially difficult if treated with respect. The original line of descent begins some way along the path from Bwlch Tryfan.

Head down the path, below the steep cliffs of Tryfan across the face of which you can detect the rising gash of the Heather Terrace, an access path onto the East Face for climbers.

Once beyond Tryfan, the path heads down to a large rock slab known as Little Tryfan (Tryfan Bach) **D**, a practice ground for novice rock climbers, though even here all the paraphernalia of rock climbing is needed.

Keep descending past Little Tryfan to reach Gwern Gof Uchaf Farm, and there turn left to walk out to reach the A5. Turn left and walk alongside the road back to Ogwen. ■

Bwlch Tryfan

Llyn Padarn

- Country park
- historic slate quarry
- dramatic castle
- lakeside path/railway

No visitor to Llanberis can fail to be impressed by the massive example of human endeavour that is portrayed in the slate quarries, a major industry in North Wales for decades. The lake is the larger of two filling the valley (the other is Llyn Peris), and its circuit is a delightful walk with outstanding views of the mountains that form the Snowdon massif.

walk **18**

Llyn Padarn, Llanberis

walk 18

START Llanberis

DISTANCE 5 miles (8km)

TIME 3 hours

PARKING Roadside car park adjoining lake

ROUTE FEATURES Slate quarries; woodland trails; lakeside paths; quiet roads

GPS WAYPOINTS
- SH 578 604
- Ⓐ SH 586 602
- Ⓑ SH 582 612
- Ⓒ SH 564 616

PUBLIC TRANSPORT Buses to Llanberis

REFRESHMENTS Cafés/pubs in Llanberis, at Slate Museum and Cwm Derwen Visitor Centre

PUBLIC TOILETS Llanberis and at country park

PLAY AREA Adjoining lake, near start

ORDNANCE SURVEY MAPS Explorer OL17 (Snowdon - Conwy Valley), Landranger 115 (Snowdon)

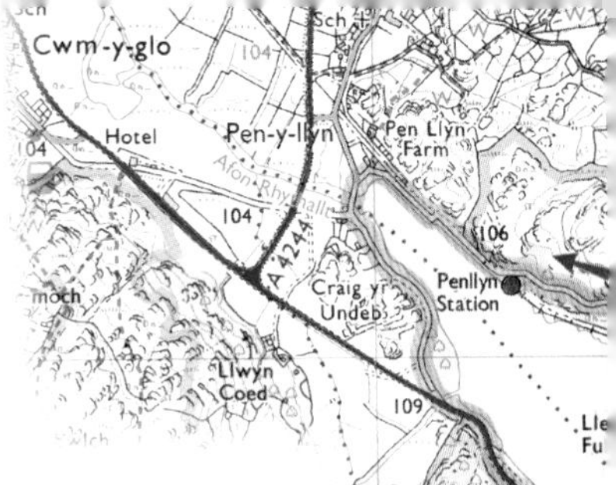

Leave the lakeside parking area and walk towards the near end of the lake. A footbridge, adjacent to a play and picnic area, gives into another car park. Keep left, following the lake edge and soon enter the Padarn Country Park at a gate.

Go forward on a grassy track to a metal kissing-gate in a fence. Maintain the same direction across the next field, and eventually reach a footbridge spanning the watery link between the two lakes.

The footbridge leads to the Welsh Slate Museum Ⓐ, and here, bear left, following the boundary of the museum towards the terminus for the Lakeside Railway.

Keep to the right of the Lake Railway buildings to locate a woodland path that leads to the V2 Incline.

Go past the Incline into woodland, soon climbing on a rocky path and passing numerous trees that are heavy with moss, to

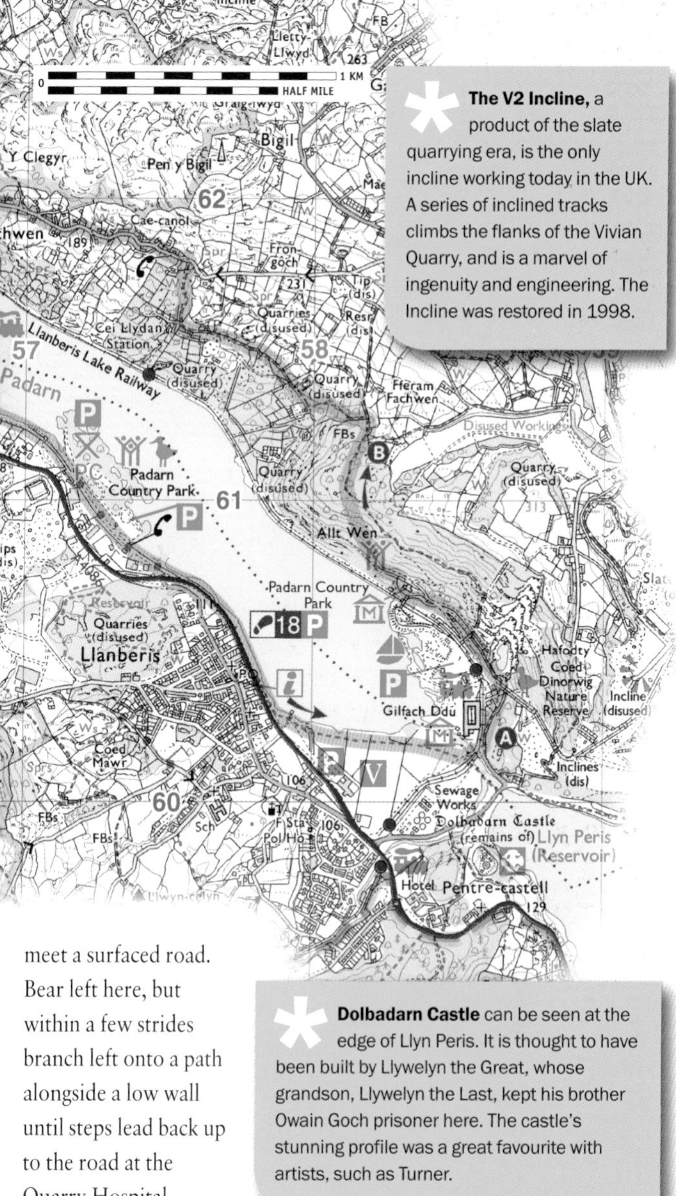

The V2 Incline, a product of the slate quarrying era, is the only incline working today in the UK. A series of inclined tracks climbs the flanks of the Vivian Quarry, and is a marvel of ingenuity and engineering. The Incline was restored in 1998.

meet a surfaced road. Bear left here, but within a few strides branch left onto a path alongside a low wall until steps lead back up to the road at the Quarry Hospital.

Dolbadarn Castle can be seen at the edge of Llyn Peris. It is thought to have been built by Llywelyn the Great, whose grandson, Llywelyn the Last, kept his brother Owain Goch prisoner here. The castle's stunning profile was a great favourite with artists, such as Turner.

Go left, passing the hospital mortuary, to re-enter woodland for what is the finest section of the walk, and follow a path across a wooded slope above Llyn Padarn. Keep an eye open for woodland birds here – nuthatch, jays, chiffchaff, willow warbler.

At a red-topped waymark pole, remain on the woodland path climbing gently with a lovely view across the lake to Llanberis, the rounded dome of Moel Eilio and, farther left, the conical summit of Yr Wyddfa (Snowdon).

? *Can you discover anything that tells you when the slate quarrying was at its most active?*

The path climbs quite high above the lake, with steep drops on the left necessitating close supervision of young children. At the high point there is a splendid view up the length of Llyn Padarn.

From here the path starts to drop steeply. When it forks, branch right, following the path to a gate near a series of low cascades embowered with birch and oak **B**.

At the gate, turn right, leaving the Padarn Country Park, and soon cross a slate bridge. Go ahead, now climbing again, on a stony track.

Around Llyn Padarn

As the rising track levels, it passes a quarry on the right and soon reaches the Cwm Derwen Woodlands and Wildlife Centre (where refreshments are seasonally available).

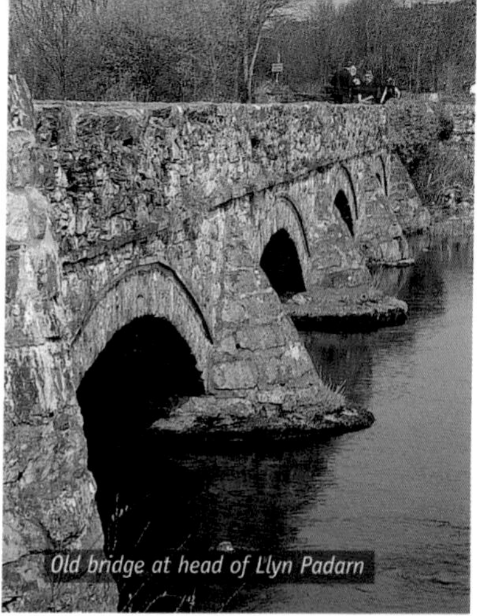
Old bridge at head of Llyn Padarn

A little distance beyond the centre the ongoing track is surfaced with concrete. As the track bends right, leave it on the apex, and go left along a narrow path to a kissing-gate giving onto a road near a telephone box. Turn left.

Now simply follow the road through the linear hamlet of Fachwen, steadily descending towards the end of Llyn Padarn. Follow the road out to a T-junction, and there turn left to cross an attractive four-arched bridge. Over the bridge, bear left to a ladder-stile giving onto an old road along the lake edge.

At the third ladder-stile, turn left onto the main valley road and walk along the roadside footpath for 450 yds, as far as a waymarked gap **C** on the left through which a path descends to the trackbed of the railway that formerly ran through the valley as far as Llanberis.

Bear left along the trackbed, taking time to check the lake for great crested grebe and goosander. Keep following the trackbed to a metal barrier (toilets nearby), and here, with a road running ahead, bear left (as if going into the car park) and then immediately right onto another wooded path parallel with the road. This path leads into the edge of another car park.

Keep on in the same direction, picking up the continuing path, and soon emerge onto the road. Go left and walk out towards the main road. Another left turn soon brings you to the end of the walk at the village car park. ■

The Miners' Track

- Lakeland scenery
- Snowdon (Yr Wyddfa)
- monster legend
- old mines

walk 19

This is a linear walk, completed in both directions, using the old track that the miners built to reach the copper mines below Snowdon. Today it is one of the most popular ways to ascend Snowdon, but this walk only goes as far as the top lake, Glaslyn, before turning round to head back for Pen-y-pass.

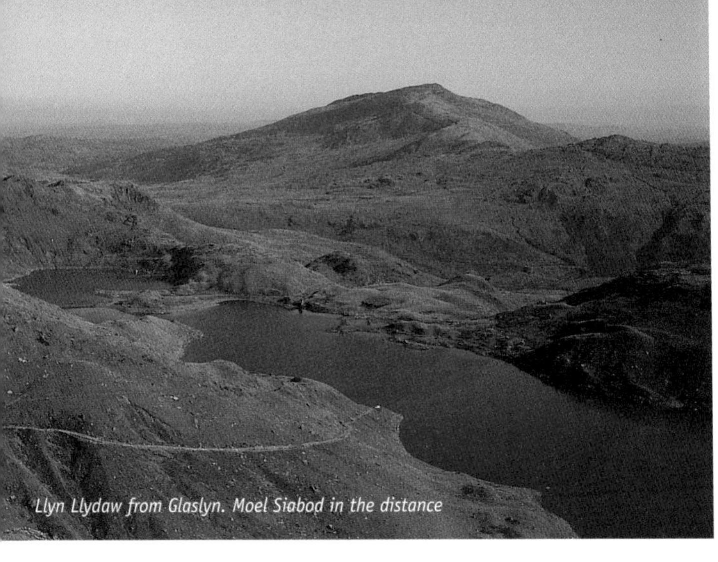

Llyn Llydaw from Glaslyn. Moel Siabod in the distance

walk 19

START Pen-y-pass

DISTANCE 5½ miles (9km)

HEIGHT GAIN 850ft (260m)

TIME 2½ hours

PARKING Pen-y-pass (Fee)

ROUTE FEATURES Mountain tracks; lakes; high mountains; mine buildings

GPS WAYPOINTS

- SH 647 555
- (A) SH 641 548
- (B) SH 634 546
- (C) SH 619 545

PUBLIC TRANSPORT Sherpa Bus Service from Nant Peris

REFRESHMENTS Pen-y-pass

PUBLIC TOILETS At start

PLAY AREA None

ORDNANCE SURVEY MAPS Explorer OL17 (Snowdon - Conwy Valley), Landranger 115 (Snowdon)

The walk begins along the broad track clearly heading away from the car park at Pen-y-pass. Go through the gate clearly marked Miners' Track, and follow the well-graded path that was originally used to bring copper down from the mines. This soon passes the first of three lakes encountered on the walk, Llyn Teyrn (A).

As the track continues, so Y Lliwedd, a twin-peaked summit, appears on the left, its steep cliffs the preserve of rock gymnasts and goats. Continue, to turn a corner and discover the largest lake, Llyn Llydaw (Britanny Lake) (B), at the far end of which the distinctive cone of Snowdon rises dramatically.

As you cross the causeway, the great red wall of Crib Goch towers above, a spectacular traverse on which many a head for heights has been put to the test. Once over the causeway, keep following the track as it follows the shore of Llyn Llydaw for a while, and then reaches a group of old mine buildings, the

Llyn Teyrn, the Lake of Ruler, occupies a shallow hollow scooped out by a glacier and is thought to have been named after a local prince. On its shores are the ruins of barracks used by the miners. Local legend has it that the barracks were occupied by French miners escaping the Napoleonic Wars.

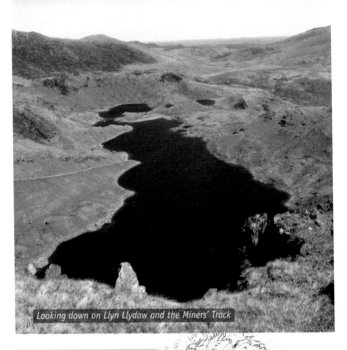

Looking down on Llyn Llydaw and the Miners' Track

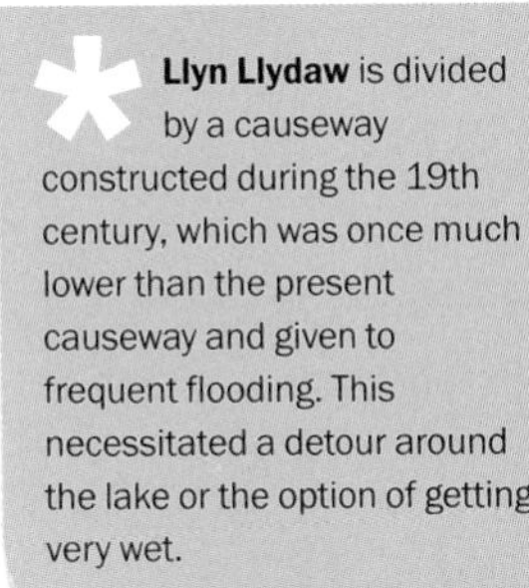

Llyn Llydaw is divided by a causeway constructed during the 19th century, which was once much lower than the present causeway and given to frequent flooding. This necessitated a detour around the lake or the option of getting very wet.

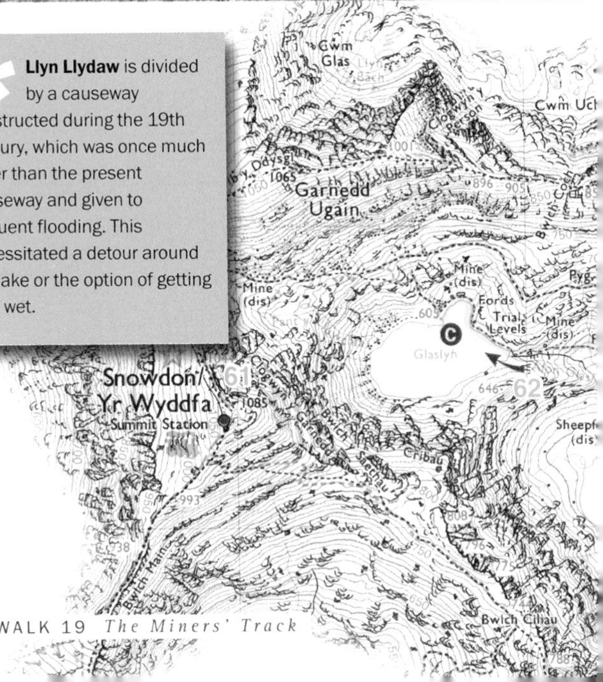

*Glaslyn was once known as Llyn y Ffynnon Las, the **Lake of the Green Fountain,** and is said to be inhabited by a monster, an *afanc*, which once lived in a pool near Betws-y-coed, but caused such havoc among the local population that they carted it by oxen to the lake below Snowdon's gaze.

main site of industrial activity in the area.

Beyond the mine buildings, the track begins to climb quite steeply, and finally reaches another lake, Glaslyn **C**, its waters tinted remarkably by copper ore.

Glaslyn has a pebble 'beach' and this makes a lovely place to have a mountain picnic before simply re-tracing your steps to Pen-y-pass. ■

? *Because of the monster in Glaslyn it is said that no bird will fly completely across the lake, and will always divert away. See if you can spot any that do.*

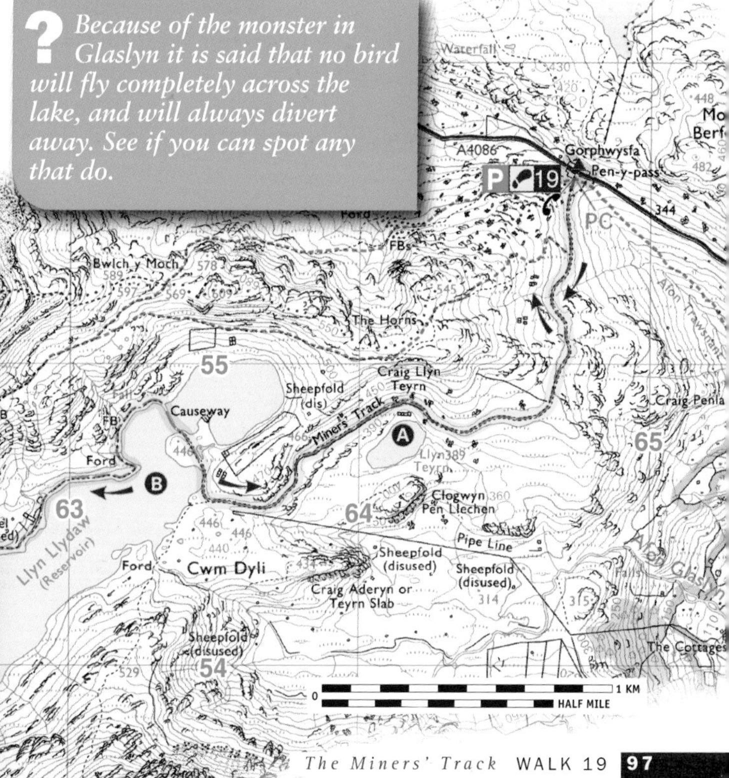

Conwy Mountain

- Estuary wildlife
- ancient hill fort
- wild ponies
- birds of prey

walk 20

Conwy Mountain provides a grandstand view of Conwy Bay, Great Orme and the eastern summits of the Snowdonia National Park. The walk begins in Conwy, the ancient stronghold of Edward I, where his castle dominates the estuary, and climbs energetically to the top of the mountain, which is topped by an ancient hill fort.

Conwy Castle and Estuary from Conwy Mountain

walk 20

START Conwy town centre

DISTANCE $5\frac{3}{4}$ miles (9.4km)

HEIGHT GAIN 885ft (270m)

TIME 3 hours

PARKING Car parks in town centre (Pay and Display)

ROUTE FEATURES Estuary; stiles; exposed hill top; muddy fields; some road walking

GPS WAYPOINTS

- Start: SH 782 776
- A SH 775 782
- B SH 770 778
- C SH 751 774
- D SH 749 770
- E SH 763 767

PUBLIC TRANSPORT Rail and bus services to Conwy

REFRESHMENTS Numerous cafés in Conwy

PUBLIC TOILETS On quayside

PLAY AREA None

ORDNANCE SURVEY MAPS Explorer OL17 (Snowdon - Conwy Valley), Landranger 115 (Snowdon)

Leave Conwy by heading onto the quayside. Turn left and shortly pass the Smallest House in Great Britain.

Continue along the quay and out through the town wall. At a road junction bear right onto the signposted North Wales Path. This becomes a pleasant surfaced path leading along the water's edge.

Follow the path to its end, at a road junction **A**, and there turn left and walk out to meet the A547, near a pedestrian crossing. Cross into the road opposite and go over a pedestrian bridge spanning the North Wales railway line. On the other side, continue along a walled track to a surfaced lane and then a road junction.

At the junction, turn right, climbing gently past houses. When the tarmac ends and the track levels, branch right to a ladder stile giving onto Conwy Mountain.

? *See if you can find a postman on horseback.*

The ongoing path climbs through bracken and is flanked by young beech and gorse. It climbs vigorously for a while with improving views south and east that embrace Conwy Castle

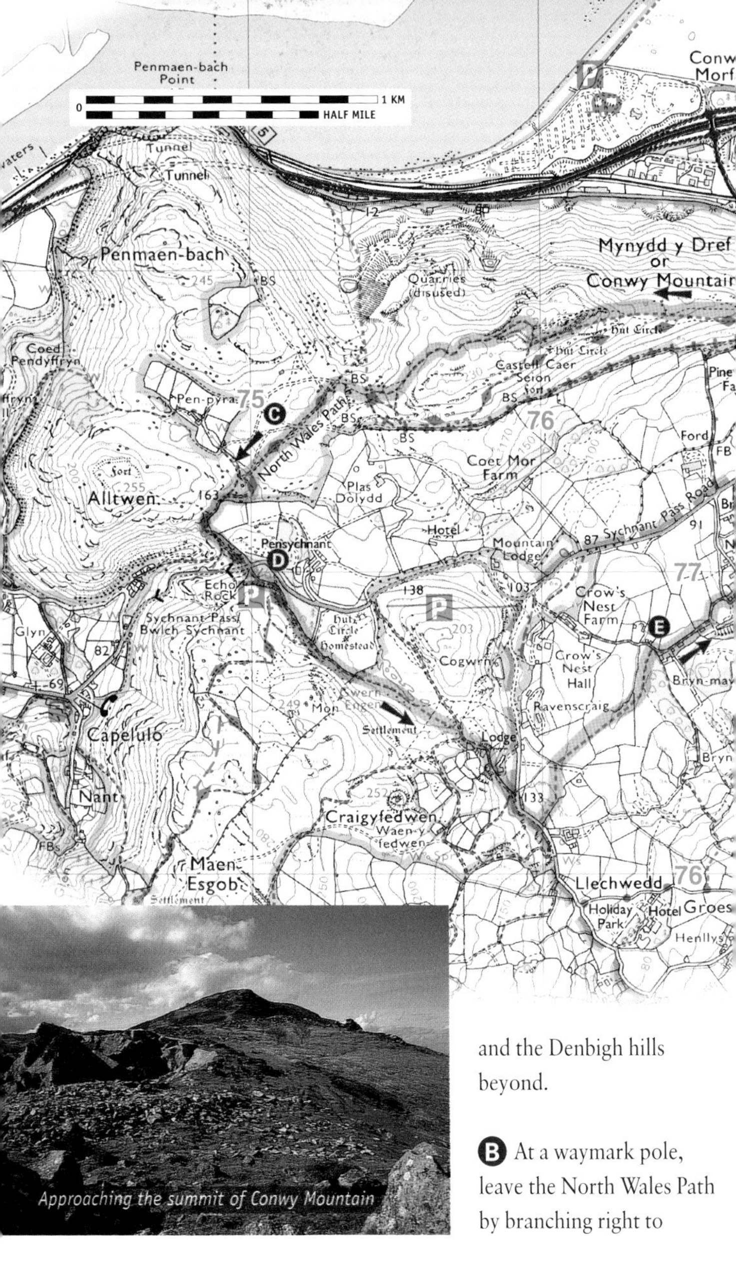

Approaching the summit of Conwy Mountain

and the Denbigh hills beyond.

B At a waymark pole, leave the North Wales Path by branching right to

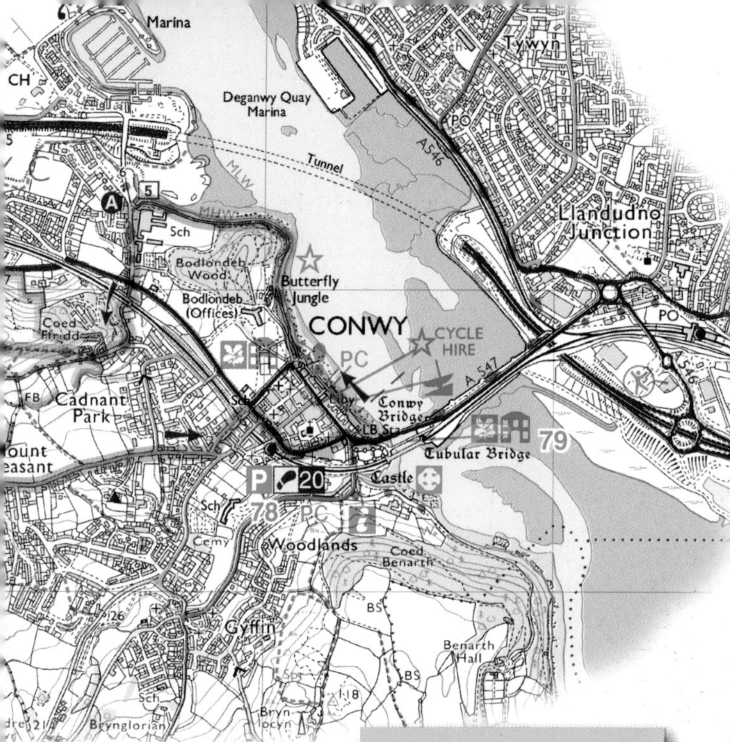

intercept a wide grassy path that runs along the spine of the mountain.

Turn left onto this and continue climbing easily; as much as possible following the path along the crest. From time to time paths appear right and left, all of which lead in the same direction, but these do not cross the top of the mountain, which involves a slight detour. Keep an eye open for feral ponies that live along the mountain.

Conwy Castle was one of a chain of 17 fortresses built by Edward I along the coast of North Wales. Castle and town were built at the same time: the castle affording protection for the town and its people, who in turn looked after the castle. Settlers came, attracted by the shrewd offer of generous conditions for trade, building and leasing. In Edward's time only the English were allowed to live within the town walls, or to run a business. The Welsh had to live outside, and could only pursue occupations as farmers or shepherds.

Continue along the top of the mountain, still following the crest path as it gradually begins to descend to thread a way through low hills at the western end of the ridge, steadily moving to the landward side of the mountain.

> * The top of **Conwy Mountain** is occupied by an ancient hill fort (Castell Caer Seion). This is a pre-Roman Iron Age settlement, which covers a good section of the mountain top.

The path comes down to meet a broad track **C** at a waymark (once more following the North Wales Path). Keep forward across the track to engage another short ascent before the Path drops to a ford and stepping stones not far south-east of Pen-pyra Farm.

Cross the farm access and either go forward onto a broad grassy track across a low shoulder, or simply turn left along the access track. Both routes rejoin on the other side of the shoulder, from where the track can be followed out to the road at the top of the Sychnant Pass **D**.

Cross the road and climb to a gate in a wall, beyond which a gently rising path runs beside a wall.

Just as the path passes beneath overhead powerlines it forks. Branch left, onto a narrow path climbing across a hill shoulder and still parallel with a wall.

Soon the path descends to a ladder-stile in a wall corner. Over this, go forward towards a small group of lakes (Gwern Engen), and keep on in the same direction to intercept another rough track. Turn right to a track junction near a group of buildings.

Now bear left and soon descend steeply on a rough track that leads to a narrow road.

Turn right, going past Ty Coch Farm. At the next house on the left (Y Bwthyn), leave the road by turning through an ornate metal kissing-gate onto an enclosed path. The path breaks out at another gate into a field. Strike across this, towards a vehicle track.

Cross the track and go through a wooden gate, and then follow an obvious route across fields linked by gates, finally targeting an oak tree in the third field. The tree stands in a fence corner not far from a small wooded hill that in springtime is bright with primroses.

Aim for a red-roofed black and white house, to the right of which another gate gives onto a lane **E**.

Turn right, following the lane past Oakwood Park Hall to a T-junction. Turn right, and 20 yds farther on go left at a signposted path. Now go forward across fields to reach a metal kissing-gate.

Hill fort on the summit of Conwy Mountain

Through the gate, bear left along the field edge to meet the Sychnant Pass Road. Turn right and follow the road back towards Conwy.

On reaching the town walls, keep right to pass through a pedestrian archway, then rejoin the main road and walk towards the town centre. At a T-junction, turn right and follow the road through the centre of Conwy towards the castle and the start. ■

Further Information

Walking Safety

Always take with you both warm and waterproof clothing and sufficient food and drink. Wear suitable footwear such as strong walking boots or shoes that give a good grip over stony ground, on slippery slopes and in muddy conditions. Try to obtain a local weather forecast and bear it in mind before you start. Do not be afraid to abandon your proposed route and return to your starting point in the event of a sudden and unexpected deterioration in the weather.

All the walks described in this book will be safe to do, given due care and respect, even during the winter. Indeed, a crisp, fine winter day often provides perfect walking conditions, with firm ground underfoot and a clarity of light unique to that time of the year.

The most difficult hazard likely to be encountered is mud, especially when walking along woodland and field paths, farm tracks and bridleways – the latter in particular can often get churned up by cyclists and horses. In summer, an additional difficulty may be narrow and overgrown paths, particularly along the edges of cultivated fields. Neither should constitute a major problem provided that the appropriate footwear is worn.

Global Positioning System (GPS)

What is GPS?

Global Positioning System, or GPS for short, is a fully-functional navigation system that uses a network of satellites to calculate positions, which are then transmitted to hand-held receivers. By

En route to Llyn Dinas

measuring the time it takes a signal to reach the receiver, the distance from the satellite can be estimated. Repeat this with several satellites and the receiver can then triangulate its position, in effect telling the receiver exactly where you are, in any weather, day or night, anywhere on Earth.

GPS information, in the form of grid reference data, is increasingly being used in Pathfinder® guidebooks, and many readers find the positional accuracy GPS affords a reassurance, although its greatest benefit comes when you are walking in remote, open countryside or through forests.

GPS has become a vital global utility, indispensable for modern navigation on land, sea and air around the world, as well as an important tool for map-making and land surveying.

Follow the Country Code

- Be safe – plan ahead and follow any signs
- Leave gates and property as you find them
- Protect plants and animals, and take your litter home
- Keep dogs under close control
- Consider other people

(Natural England)

Useful Organisations

Cadw: Welsh Assembly Government
Plas Carew, Unit 5/7 Cefn Coed,
Parc Nantgarw, Cardiff
CF15 7QQ
Tel: 01443 336000
www.cadw.wales.gov.uk

Coed Cymru,
The Old Sawmill, Tregynon,
Newtown, Powys SY16 3PL
Tel: 01686 650777
www.coedcymru.org.uk

Campaign for the Protection of Rural Wales
Ty Gwyn, 31 High Street,
Welshpool, Powys SY21 7YD
Tel: 01938 552525
www.cprw.org.uk

Countryside Council for Wales
Maes-y-Ffynnon,
Penrhosgarnedd, Bangor,
Gwynedd LL57 2DW
Tel: 0845 130 6229
www.ccw.gov.uk

National Trust Office for Wales
Trinity Square, Llandudno,
Gwynedd LL30 2DE
Tel: 01492 860123
www.nationaltrust.org.uk

North Wales Wildlife Trust
376 High Street, Bangor,
Gwynedd LL57 1YE
Tel: 01248 351541
www.northwaleswildlifetrust.org.uk

Ordnance Survey
Romsey Road, Maybush,
Southampton SO16 4GU
Tel. 08456 05 05 05 (Lo-call)
www.ordnancesurvey.co.uk

Ramblers' Association
2nd Floor, Camelford House,
87-90 Albert Embankment,

London SE1 7TW
Tel. 020 7339 8500
www.ramblers.org.uk

Royal Society for the Protection of Birds (RSPB)
The Lodge, Sandy, Beds SG19 2DL
Tel. 01767 680551
www.rspb.org.uk

Tourist Information

Aberdyfi: 01654 767321
Bala: 01678 521021
Barmouth: 01341 280787
Betws-y-coed: 01690 710426
Conwy: 01492 592248
Corris: 01654 761244
Dolgellau: 01341 422888
Llanberis: 01286 870765

Travel Information

Bus Traveline
0870 608 2608
National Rail Enquiries
08457 48 49 50
www.thetrainline.com

Tryfan south ridge from Bwlch Tryfan

Ordnance Survey Maps

Explorers

OL17 (Snowdon and Conwy Valley)

OL18 (Harlech, Porthmadog & Bala)

OL23 (Cadair Idris & Llyn Tegid)

Landrangers

115 (Snowdon)

124 (Porthmadog & Dolgellau)

125 (Bala & Lake Vyrnwy)

135 (Aberystwyth & Machynlleth)

Answers to Questions

Walk 1: It was erected to mark the reputed birthplace on the shores of Llyn Geirionydd of Taliesin the chief bard of the 6th-century, a contemporary, it is said, of the Wizard Merlin.

Craig y Bere

Walk 2: The grey wagtail is almost always found near water. They like to perch on rocks in the streams, and it is usually their wagging tail that catches the eye.

Walk 3: A plaque near the road junction on the return part of the walk explains that Dulwich College Plot was planted during evacuation to the area in 1941.

Walk 4: Carn March Arthur, above the Dyfi Estuary, is a rock imprinted, it is said, with the hoofprint of the horse that carried King Arthur to safety by leaping across the Dyfi Estuary as he was pursued by enemies. It is marked by a slate standing stone and stands beside the track.

Walk 5: Between October 1992 and July 1995. The information is found in the church.

Walk 6: Above the falls and over the ladder-stile, the mixed woodland contains many young trees of the kind popularly used at Christmas.

Walk 7: The weather.

Walk 8: Wheatear are summer visitors from Africa. The females arrive first: they are buff coloured; then the males arrive. Males are slaty blue in colour.

Walk 9: The ring ouzel frequents rocky terrain like Cwm Idwal, but is difficult to spot. Look for them among the boulders below Twll Du.

Walk 10: There are different species of spruce here, as well as lodgepole pine. Each has a different cone.

Walk 11: Glaslyn Bridge in Beddgelert was built in 1951 at the Glaslyn Foundry in Porthmadog.

Walk 12: Holly. Wherever you find holly trees like this along ancient tracks, it lends support to the suggestion that this may have been a drove road, since the tree provided a rough form of feed for cattle.

Walk 13: Forty. The information is contained on a panel near the mill site.

Walk 14: There are at least seven, but it sometimes seems like there are more because the same hill is viewed from a different angle.

Llyn Gwernan and Tyrau Mawr

Walk 15: The gold was used to fashion Royal wedding rings. The information is on a panel alongside the estuary.

Walk 16: Only at busy times are all nine likely to be in use. Four of the steam locomotives were built in 1985/96, and one in 1922.

Walk 17: Meadow pipits are almost as abundant in the mountains as they are in meadows, and are often found in association with the summer-visiting wheatears.

Walk 18: 1875-1930s. At the V2 Incline, an information panel reads: 'The incline was used from 1875 until the early 1930s, during the peak of slate production around Llanberis'.

Walk 19: Everything depends on whether you believe legends, or the fact that birds seldom fly in a straight line!

Walk 20: There is one on the letterbox built into the wall of the Boat House, just outside Conwy town wall.